UNMASKING PREJUDICE
Silencing the Internal Voice of Bigotry

By: Dr. Melodye Hilton

D1637219

UNMASKING PREJUDICE: SILENCING THE INTERNAL VOICE OF BIGOTRY

Copyright © 2019 Atlantic Publishing Group, Inc.

1405 SW 6th Avenue • Ocala, Florida 34471 • Phone 352-622-1825 • Fax 352-622-1875
Website: www.atlantic-pub.com • Email: sales@atlantic-pub.com
SAN Number: 268-1250

All rights reserved. No part of this publication may be reproduced, stored in a retrieval system, or transmitted in any form or by any means, electronic, mechanical, photocopying, recording, scanning, or otherwise, except as permitted under Section 107 or 108 of the 1976 United States Copyright Act, without the prior written permission of the publisher and Dr. Melodye Hilton. Requests to the Publisher for permission should be sent to Atlantic Publishing Group, Inc., 1405 SW 6th Avenue, Ocala, Florida 34471. Requests to the author for permissions should be sent to contact@DrMelodye.com.

Library of Congress Cataloging-in-Publication Data

Names: Hilton, Melodye, 1955- author.
Title: Unmasking prejudice : silencing the internal voice of bigotry / Dr. Melodye Hilton.
Description: Ocala, Florida : Atlantic Publishing Group, Inc., [2019]
Identifiers: LCCN 2018057565| ISBN 9781620236321 (pbk.) | ISBN 162023632X
Subjects: LCSH: Prejudices.
Classification: LCC HM1091 .H55 2019 | DDC 303.3/85—dc23
LC record available at https://lccn.loc.gov/2018057565

LIMIT OF LIABILITY/DISCLAIMER OF WARRANTY: The publisher and the author make no representations or warranties with respect to the accuracy or completeness of the contents of this work and specifically disclaim all warranties, including without limitation warranties of fitness for a particular purpose. No warranty may be created or extended by sales or promotional materials. The advice and strategies contained herein may not be suitable for every situation. This work is sold with the understanding that the publisher is not engaged in rendering legal, accounting, or other professional services. If professional assistance is required, the services of a competent professional should be sought. Neither the publisher nor the author shall be liable for damages arising herefrom. The fact that an organization or Web site is referred to in this work as a citation and/or a potential source of further information does not mean that the author or the publisher endorses the information the organization or Web site may provide or recommendations it may make. Further, readers should be aware that Internet Web sites listed in this work may have changed or disappeared between when this work was written and when it is read.

The life experiences of the contributors are a documentation of their individual stories and personal encounters. Neither the author nor the publisher assumes responsibility for the accuracy of these accounts or for any offensive language contained therein. Used by permission.

TRADEMARK DISCLAIMER: All trademarks, trade names, or logos mentioned or used are the property of their respective owners and are used only to directly describe the products being provided. Every effort has been made to properly capitalize, punctuate, identify, and attribute trademarks and trade names to their respective owners, including the use of ® and ™ wherever possible and practical. Atlantic Publishing Group, Inc. is not a partner, affiliate, or licensee with the holders of said trademarks.

Interior artwork and images are the sole property of Dr. Melodye Hilton, Hilton Consulting, LLC

Printed in the United States

PROJECT MANAGER: Katie Cline
INTERIOR LAYOUT, COVER, AND JACKET DESIGN: Nicole Sturk

ENDORSEMENTS

I doubt there is a person alive who has not been on both ends of the whipping stick of prejudice — as either the whipper or the whipee — at some point in their life.

Prejudice is part of the human condition, but it's a part of us that has it roots in the lowest, most reptilian part of us. Prejudice is the eighth deadly sin, and the future of the human race will be determined by the degree to which we can individually and collectively unmask and eradicate its devastating influence.

There are stories in this book — real stories of and by real people — that will break your heart, make you mad, inspire you to act, or even reveal a darkness within your own spirit that you didn't know you had. By unmasking the reality of prejudice and injustice in the world and in our own hearts, and by recognizing how much it imprisons us all, we can begin a journey to greater freedom for all.

Dr. Melodye is a torchbearer of freedom and a trumpeter of possibility for what we can be and become as individuals and as a global society. While she shines her light on the evils of bigotry, prejudice, and injustice, she also reveals a pathway to a better life and a better world.

Dr. Melodye writes:

> Throughout history we see iconic men and women standing for justice. What we do not always see, however, are the countless unsung heroes who take on the personal responsibility to respond to injustices when they hear a cry for help.
>
> We may not be able to change the whole world, but we might just be able to change our world — our family, our field, our community, even our nation.

And as Margaret Mead wrote: "Never doubt that a small group of thoughtful, committed citizens can change the world; indeed, it's the only thing that ever has."

Will you choose to be one of them?

Peter Demarest
Author, "Answering The Central Question"
Co-Founder& President of Axiogenics, LLC
and the Self-Leadership Institute

Dr. Melodye Hilton is well-equipped and qualified to write this book on Unmasking Prejudice. As a professional who has traveled internationally for over 35 years and served in non-profit organizations as founder, leader, mentor, and coach, Dr. Hilton has interacted with and served many diverse populations of people. Her passion for justice in societies of the world has propelled her to write this phenomenal book exposing the prejudice and bias that is hidden within all of us.

As a professional counselor for over 20 years and as a recently retired Army colonel with over 34 years leadership experience, I can attest to the insightful ability demonstrated by Dr. Hilton to unmask prejudice in our lives and in society. Of the resources that are available today, this book is greatly needed to unmask areas of prejudice to encourage and promote healthy relationships.

In her book "Unmasking Prejudice", Dr. Hilton discusses societal issues and personal perspectives that reveal hidden areas of prejudice that influence people in every walk of life. Her ability to provide the insight needed and to reveal the hidden dynamics that lead to personal prejudice enables the reader to recognize and overcome bias and prejudice that influences every part of their life.

Dr. Hilton concludes her discussion on unmasking prejudice by reminding the reader that contrary to prejudice, love is a powerful force. She reminds that reader that because love never fails, it has the power to counteract every form of prejudice and bias.

She challenges the reader to conduct introspection to unmask the hidden darkness that lies within us in order to bring forth the truth in love that all humankind has value. This book is a must read for all those who have a passion for truth and justice within our self and our society.

Linda R. Herbert
PhD, Counseling Education & Supervision
Colonel, United States Army (Retired)

Dr. Melodye Hilton is a living example of someone who lives out a leadership style of love, empowerment, and validation. Her heart of love and her fight for justice permeates every page of this book.

"Unmasking Prejudice: Silencing the Internal Voice of Bigotry" is an ocean of applicable information and principled truths that will enrich you, the reader.

The wealth of the book is its ability to impact the human soul in such a way that we can't ever again live our lives ignorant of a vicious saboteur that silently, and often times freely, lurks around the halls of our minds, sabotaging our internal world and thus affecting our chances of success externally in more than one way.

If you're like me, prior to reading this book you had never ACTIVELY thought of the impact that prejudice has over our societies, families, relationships, and our own personal lives. If I'm being honest, I didn't think prejudice was affecting me at all. It was, perhaps, another evil that I knew existed, but didn't quite grasp just how much it may actually be affecting our relationships and opportunities for successful partnerships.

Through the reading of this book, you will come to understand how prejudice may be negatively impacting you, your success, your relationships, and your ability to produce positive change in your sphere of influence. This book will equip you with the tools necessary to identify where the voice of bigotry lies, and it will empower you to confront and deal with this resident evil in a manner that is empowering both for you and others.

Adonay De Los Santos
Owner, Adonay De Los Santos Translation Services
Managua, Nicaragua

Prejudices can shape one's world and make it hard to fully see the potential in others around them because of race, gender, economical class, religious beliefs, etc. A person's view of others can often be based off of a negative experience, what was instilled into them as a child, or ignorance of the value that can be found in others. It is very important to recognize our perceptions, attitudes, and behaviors as they relate to others to really hone in on our unconscious negative biases towards others.

In "Unmasking Prejudice", Dr. Melodye Hilton explains how non-confronted prejudices can bring injustice to so many around us and it keeps us from embracing so many around us. With her unequivocal and thought-provoking written words to change our generation, she not only initiates a call to action, but she models how it can be done. While reading this book, you will ask yourself am I a part of the solution or the problem? Have I taken the steps to unmask my own mindsets? After reading the book, you will discover how to be the solution, and have keys to assist you with tearing down mindsets that hinder community, partnership, and acceleration.

What a powerful tool that will assist in raising instruments of justice. Dr. Melodye has a strong mandate to encourage all those with whom she comes in contact to use their power for good. She is a living testament of how impactful this principle can be.

Harold Williams
AVP - Wells Fargo Bank & Co. (Loan Operations)
Senior Leader- Activation International, Inc.

This book is dedicated to Steven, Rebecca, Joel, Erin, Ayden, Laila, and Maxwell, who all remind me that posterity is our greatest wealth.

TABLE OF CONTENTS

FOREWORD

It is not often that I come upon a book that I see as essential and important. It is even more rare that I find a book whose author is not just teaching others new thoughts, perceptions, and attitudes, but also offering her own life, her own experiences, mistakes, and negative stories and insights into personal wrong thinking and wrong actions. This book is a transparent narrative of a life worthy of emulation.

Melodye has captured an essential human capacity for this moment in history: the ability to 'walk in another person's shoes.' She encourages each reader to live a life committed to the validation of others, the lifting of self and others into the light of empathy, compassion, and learning to be the presence of love, rather than seeking to be loved.

This book, "Unmasking Prejudice...", is important at this moment of time in the United States. Divisiveness, condemnation of others, and insensitivity to the humanity of individuals is all too omnipresent. Our political leaders — or social mouthpieces — our biased rhetoric, is so full of untruth, exaggerated accusations, and vitriol that it's hard for all of us to find moments of silence, so we can hear our humanity calling out to us. We have within ourselves, without exception, a human adult, whose life is valuable, whose contribution is needed, and whose participation will be welcome and meaningful.

Melodye provides, in this book, a clarion call for us to listen to this adult voice that exists in each of us and to decide — one day, one experience, one moment, and one person at a time — to be someone who chooses to be the presence of love, wisdom, and real contributory power and knowledge for our own sake, for the sake of others, for the sake of lifting humanity.

I applaud Melodye's life, lived with personal courage, heartfelt actions, and teaching. She makes me want to live my life at this more adult human being level of engagement. And I say here now, Melodye, I will do whatever work it takes for me to become the presence of humanity that you have so thoughtfully and humbly described. Thank you. I am lifted up by your words and the gifts of your life disclosures.

Lynn Taylor, President
Taylor Protocols, Inc.

INTRODUCTION

There are many individuals of influence walking the streets, sitting in boardrooms, enacting legislation, teaching our children, or interacting within culture in a multitude of ways. Knowingly or unknowingly, many of these leaders are wearing masks that are hiding various types of prejudice. Prejudice is simply *pre-judgment,* as assumptions are made without accurate information, opinions are formed without facts, and beliefs are established without truth. All prejudice is destructive and based on fear-based attitudes that affect relationships and partnerships and sabotage the ability to lead with justice, honor, and validation.

Leadership is the influence that we carry in our spheres of responsibility. We cannot lead effectively if we carry any form of prejudice within our internal dialogue. When leadership decisions are made through a grid of fear-based bias or an attitude of supremacy, they will be, for all intents and purposes, defective and the outcomes flawed.

When a leader *silences the internal voice of bigotry* constructing decisions for the good of all, their leadership decisions will be fundamentally pure and the outcomes favorable for the individual and the corporate good. Essentially, this has the intrinsic ability to bring healing to many and establish structures that will help to heal our land.

There is great power and responsibility associated with any form of leadership influence. Whether you are a school student influencing your peers, a friend, spouse, parent, teacher, actor, athlete, spiritual leader, businessperson, or politician, there is a vital mandate to lead impartially. Wherever there is a platform of influence, there is an ability to persuade either for good or for harm.

Negative experiences have marked all of us — every single person on the planet. These experiences pressure us internally and profile our beliefs about different groups of people. Whether it be age, race, gender, socio-economic status, political views, or position in society, our tendency is to group people together and pre-judge everyone based upon external narratives, the views of our closest relationships, and/or our personal history.

Many years ago, I was an indignantly passionate *man-hater* supporting the woman's liberation movement of the 1970s. To me it was not about equal rights for women. That was only how it appeared; it was my mask. My true goal rather, was to emerge as *greater* than all men. This was prejudice that was seeded into the soil of my soul as a young girl who experienced repeated encounters of sexual molestation. Within the hidden motives of my heart, I did not fight for the noble cause of equality for woman. Instead, I secretly wanted the injury of all men believing that they were all perpetrators.

> *Each person is an individual — it is unfair to judge someone through your past experiences with others.*

Every type of prejudice, bias, or racism is self-sabotage! I was horribly deceived by the pain of my past, which impeded my emotional health and my ability to find internal peace and purpose. I am so grateful that those days are behind me.

> *I cannot remove painful past experiences, but I can refuse their power to control my decisions.*

Scientifically speaking, every thought we accept establishes memory within the neuro-networking of our brain. It is impossible to devalue, hate, disrespect, degrade, or demonstrate prejudice toward another without it causing a feedback effect into our very own memory. Whether our prejudicial actions are obvious, subtle, or covertly infusing our thought processes, it is in the long run *self*-destructive. It is time to remove the mask of outward pretense and arise with genuine validation for one another! It is impossible to be critical, judgmental, unforgiving, or gossip-mongering when we authentically value and honor others.

> *The validation of the human soul cannot co-exist with prejudice, injustice, or discrimination of any kind.*

Thomas Jefferson said, "The care of human life and happiness, and not their destruction, is the first and only objective of good government." Truly, this should be the objective of every honorable man or woman, especially those who aspire to lead well.

Let us challenge ourselves to silence the covert thoughts of bigotry that we have allowed to occupy our minds. Every leader who genuinely desires to see our land healed must boldly choose validation, honor, respect, hope, and peace. This decision will not only impact our own emotional health, but sanction healthy perspectives in the words we speak and the decisions we make.

> *Every thought I entertain is a seed of destiny — for good or harm.*

It's time to take off the masks of pretense and choose to genuinely value all of humanity. Let us utilize our emotional energies to influence generations to live well, love much, and believe for the best. Let our revolutionary voices of validation be heard. This is a cause worth living for!

CHAPTER ONE
The Unmasking

The truth is that we all wear masks — whether consciously or subconsciously. In the same way that our closets are filled with a variety of clothing in styles for every occasion, we put on different facades that serve us in every type of environment. From the time we are small children, we focus on doing whatever necessary to get our needs met. Think about a baby who cries when he or she needs some type of care. From birth, we are learning how our actions produce a response. If we enjoy that response, we repeat the action over and over again to bring about favorable results. We learn what to do and what not to do in order to get what we want. Likewise, we also learn to adapt or modify ourselves within our surroundings so that we are accepted and celebrated. After all, the core need of every human being is to be loved and to belong.

As we mature, we begin to recognize that, while keeping some thoughts unsaid is wise, wearing a facade to cover our true selves is actually counterproductive to our internal health. In trying to meet our own needs, many times we sabotage healthy relationships in the process. We construct emotional walls that we believe will protect us, but meanwhile they also *prevent* us from making a difference in the lives of others. We remain self-focused, closed-handed, and closed-hearted rather than living generously to serve those around us. The desire to add value to our world is woven into the very fabric of our humanity. However, when conflict comes, we subconsciously step into the survival instinct of self-preservation. Our beliefs and our actions then often become self-serving and ego-driven. We subtly learn what masks we need to wear in order to self-fortify and protect ourselves.

One of the most destructive masks that we can wear is the mask of prejudice. This mask is nefarious as it hides a perverse agenda that devalues others and postures us to be instruments of injustice.

In order to remove this mask, we must first come to terms with the reason why we would go to such great lengths to wear it in the first place.

The Pretense Behind the Mask

I define a *mask* as something that hides the internal reality of an individual's thoughts or character from others. The mask portrays the message that we want people to hear but isn't necessarily the truth. Imagine people knowing your every thought or emotion; think about the times you are with a group of people and you think, "I wish I could leave right now." "I'm so tired; I just want to go home!" "What an ugly outfit." "This person really irritates me!" "Wow, they are really overweight … the buttons are ready to pop off their shirt!"

What if others could hear our prejudiced thoughts? "That person is racist, I can tell by the way they looked at me." "The only reason that guy got a promotion was because the company needed to check off their minority box." "Women need to be put in their place … at home where they belong!" "That man is a pervert … they all are." "Didn't that kid learn to be seen and not heard?" "That homeless man is just too lazy to work." "That old executive needs to retire; he has nothing more to contribute."

Hopefully you are mature enough to rein in your tongue and not allow those inappropriate words to spew out of your mouth. The old adage is applicable, "If you can't say something nice, don't say anything at all."[1] What is better, however, is to stop hiding behind the mask of pretense while *patting yourself on the back* for your developed restraint. In reality, what is needed is to face up to the fear and ignorance of those thoughts and *silence the internal voice of bigotry*. The courageous internal choice is to not allow access to those thoughts, attitudes, or mindsets.

Some wear masks of silence in the name of political correctness. Others wear masks of protest in the name of activism. We become hypersensitive and quickly offended reactors. Subsequently, we internally subscribe to beliefs that are harmful to our emotional health. Our masks keep us from building bridges of healthy relationships and enjoying the beauty of diverse connections.

> *Words and their corresponding actions have amazing power. They plant seeds for good or harm, hope or fear. They have the ability to either hurt or heal, to alienate or embrace.*

Masks to Manipulate

All manipulation is self-focused and fundamentally deceptive. It appears and acts in such a way as to disguise the truth. Manipulative words may be sweet to the ears, but the heart's motives are premeditatedly corrupt. While what is said and done may appear noble, in actuality it is misleading and selfish. Someone wearing this mask may appear to do good yet secretly hide an unprincipled prejudicial agenda or immoral motive.

There are two types of manipulative masks one may wear. One is subconscious while the other is deliberate. Subconscious actions are compelled by one's own lack to fill the emptiness within them. Perhaps someone has a psychological need for love and affection or even a physical need to sustain their livelihood (food, rent, etc.). The need itself is not wrong. However, when one wears a mask of manipulation, half-truths, exaggeration, or even pity — even inadvertently at times — the singular objective is compelled by lack and neediness. Interestingly enough, when we observe cultural trends in beliefs and behaviors, they often reflect society's unmet core needs.

> *The more we focus on our personal needs, the less we care for the needs of others.*

Intentional manipulation uncovers a deliberate agenda to take from someone else anything that benefits them with no regard to the pain, suffering, or loss of others. This person's flattering words set a trap; sweet-tasting promises become toxic, and his/her charming personality proves to be lethal.

My friends, Peter and Dorothée Widmer, lead a non-governmental organization (NGO) in Zürich, Switzerland. Their main purpose is to reach out to those who have been sex-trafficked or trapped within the industry. I personally have walked the streets with them in Zürich where over 4,000 sex slaves continue to be exploited. Peter shared with me about "loverboys", men who pretend to have a love attachment to a young girl to allure her into prostitution. They approach the girls in front of schools, at parties, at shopping centers, or on the internet. They shower them with compliments and presents. Then, as soon as the girls have completely fallen "in love" with their new boyfriend, the men show their *true colors*.[2]

Through the sex-trafficker's mask of manipulation, we witness a demonstration of one of the greatest evils on the planet! Many people live on a lesser scale of manipulation, but nonetheless, it still demonstrates the manipulator's lack of value for the person he desires to mislead.

In a society in which there is an epidemic of mistrust, we can be a part of the solution. We can choose to assess our hearts, remove the masks, and confront any hidden agendas within ourselves. We can learn to care deeply for the human soul and lead with integrity. When we do what is right in our unseen private world, we will live a life in which our actions courageously align with the purity of our heart. This is integrity!

A powerful principle of life reveals that the culture *within* us will indeed shape the culture *around* us. Therefore, when we walk with an internal peace, we can and will bring peace to our external world. We will not be afraid to live without a mask because we know that we are *not* manipulators or deceivers. It is liberating to be comfortable in our own skin knowing that our thoughts, attitudes, and actions are without prejudice and manipulation.

Masks of Performance

Different cultural settings expect its members to perform in a subscribed way. The mask of performance is worn to generate relational or cultural acceptance in our sphere of influence. However, it may be a false representation of who we actually are. This type of mask could be called "people-pleasing" or "appeasement." Just as an actor plays a role and aligns with the script, the character they are playing is not a true reflection of their real-life identity. Someone may play a role or act in such a way that would cause them to appear kind and good, when in actuality they are angry and do not value those around them. For appearances' sake, we can wear a public mask and perform like an actor on a movie set without a genuine expression of our true motivations.

We can be a part of the solution! When we confront our own masks of performance, we have the freeing satisfaction of no longer pretending in order to cover up our true selves. We can take a deep breath and let it out, knowing that our actions line up with our heart. This is the sweetness of being genuine and real rather than the bitter taste of realizing we've been faking it for far too long. It's time for unpretentious love and validation that helps to heal people and nations. We won't have to pretend with others when we know we're being true with ourselves. This is the honesty that will chip away at prejudice as we see ourselves, and others, for who they really are, rather than our preconceived ideas based upon things that aren't real. It is the kind of purity that will influence our world for good.

Masks of Self-Protection

The mask of self-protection is probably the greatest reason that masks are worn in the first place. After all, no one likes to feel defenseless or unsafe. We don't wear a mask of self-protection so that we can hurt someone; on the contrary, we wear it so that we ourselves do not get hurt. The motivation is survival. Every person is wired for love and validation, and when those things are withheld, or a fear exists that they will be withheld, self-protection becomes the defensive weapon (mask) of choice. When I am not accepted, I will choose this mask in order to belong. When I feel I am not good enough, I choose self-protection to hide my sense of inadequacy. When I feel others looking down on me, I wear the mask of self-protection to pretend I do not care about what they think. All the while, beneath my mask, I am hurting inside.

The negative power of the self-protective mask is that it keeps someone from crossing the unchartered territory of authenticity and true creative expression. The fear of vulnerability is too strong. This mask can be worn for so long that our bias toward others rejects anything or anyone that would contradict our internal belief of prejudice. Withdrawal or isolation may drive us to a place of perceived safety while we make assumptions about others that may or may not be true.

These masks often bring temporary results as people assume our external actions are a true representation of our hearts. This, however, does not remove the endless internal battle: "If they knew the real me…"

It becomes difficult to enjoy our relationships when we know that others are only responding to what we allow them to see while we constantly expend effort to hide the rest. Fear of rejection and abandonment keep this self-protective mask pasted to a false identity that convinces us that to lose this mask would be to lose ourselves. Over time, our voice, passions, dreams, and hopes are unrecognizable, buried so deep that we forget they even existed.

Courage to Remove the Masks

Unmasking is a courageous act! As the mask — the façade, the false reality — is removed, we see our world and ourselves through a different lens. We may discover that some of the people in our lives are only there because they relate to our masked selves; they fit into our preconceived stereotypical *box* and want to keep us there. We will also, however, discover the individuals who see us and celebrate us for who we truly are. When we stop complying to a false identity, it opens up our lives to be powerful and courageous and to celebrate and validate both ourselves *and* others. We are emancipated when masks are removed because we become independent

thinkers in our spheres of influence without pretense or egotistical agendas. We are free to care for others and allow them to care for us. We are free to trust the trustworthy and place healthy boundaries with those who prove themselves to be dishonest or devious. We see people as individuals, not as clones of a few angry voices. We are able to value others even if they do not value us. We prevail because peace rules our inner man, not the prejudice or narrow-mindedness of another. We become powerful in our ability to separate ourselves from our past experiences as we make healthy choices for our present and future. We recognize that the removal of a mask empowers us to be a positive influence in our world.

Charles Spurgeon, a preacher in the 1800s, made a statement that rings true more than 100 years later, "Sincerity makes the very least person to be of more value than most talented hypocrite."[3]

Your voice is your contribution to the world. You carry a beautiful and unique expression. Do not mask it! Recognize that your life will draw those who will celebrate, embrace, and invite your influence. Do not cover the treasure you possess!

Don't divide your energy or focus by chasing those who do not desire your portion; you are not designed to meet the need of everyone, and you won't be celebrated by everyone on the planet. Your personal success is not based upon the quantity, but the quality of contribution you bring.

> *Your success could very well be, and probably is, through partnership with someone completely different than you.*

Albert Einstein said, "The value of a man should be seen in what he gives and not in what he is able to receive."[4]

CHAPTER TWO
Pre-judgment and Assumption

Sometimes I feel like a type of crusader wielding my written and verbal *sword* against prejudice. My earliest memories of anger, frustration, even activism, were fighting against all types of prejudice, injustice, and corruption. As an idealistic 18-year-old, convinced that I could change the world, I packed my bags and moved to Washington, D.C. to work for the FBI's laboratory division. This young alpha *women's-libber* fought for every cause that stirred *righteous* indignation (which was just about everything). Those years of my life proved to be a lot of zeal without wisdom. However, as I have matured, I have not abandoned my innate passion to fight for what is right — and prejudice is inherently wrong!

The substance of prejudice is simply pre-judgment or assumption about something or someone without facts or evidence. Prejudice moves beyond race to include gender, religion, generational stereotypes, and more. It involves emotionally charged, biased opinions, ideologies, or worldviews that ultimately divide and cause emotional suffering.

As leaders, we influence and reproduce who we are into others. Where we indulge, we will see those who follow us overindulge. Parents influence their children, teachers influence their students, spiritual leaders influence believers, peers influence their friends … and so it goes. We must understand that we are conveying a persuasive message to everyone in our spheres of influence. If we think, believe, and act discriminatorily toward people who are different from us, we are propagating prejudice.

Emotional health flourishes within the beneficiary of love, validation, celebration, understanding, and inclusion. Our world, however, appears to be sliding into a deeper abyss of hatred, intolerance, pre-judgment, and division. The result is fear-based emotional instability and volatility. The ability to disagree agreeably, respect another's perspective, and empathetically take the time to understand is rapidly becoming a lost art. The end result is creating more enemies as our circle of friends gets smaller and smaller.

Prejudice may never cease in our world, but we, as leaders, must address this injustice by modeling a higher standard of honor and compassion toward our fellow man. For the most part, there is a propensity to be critical of what we do not understand; therefore, let us gain understanding of the sources of pre-judgment.

Our Family of Origin

Our family of origin models the way before us with underlying worldviews, mindsets, and what they have embraced from their forefathers. I grew up in a small, white, German community in Pennsylvania. I don't remember meeting a person of color until I was 16 years old. I am so thankful that my family was never racially prejudiced that I was aware of. In fact, I asked my grandmother what she would think if I married a black man. Her response touched my heart, "I don't care what color he is as long as he is a good Christian man." Her Christian beliefs caused her to view everyone based upon their character and not by the color of their skin. Though I was not a Christian and still a *work in progress,* her perspective helped to reinforce a healthy racial perspective within me. My grandmother was a loving and selfless woman who was always serving others. I never heard her speak a negative word about anyone! She had a lot of difficulties in her life, but you would have never known it by her attitudes, words, or actions. What a legacy!

Now, hypothetically, let's imagine if she *were* an angry racist. What if bigoted words spewed out of her mouth throughout my entire childhood? How would those words have shaped my thoughts, emotions, attitudes, beliefs, and actions?

If all of our emotional energies were invested into validating rather than criticizing, gratitude rather than complaining, and hope rather than fear, we would love life.

Teaching and Training

We are constantly being educated through both formal and informal settings — whether intentionally or inadvertently. Educators have a massive platform of influence to shape the minds of a generation. When educators proselytize rather than educate, they are promoting their personal bias, swaying the students toward *what* to think rather than teaching them *how* to think independently. Rehearsing the ideologies of a teacher in order to earn the required grade stifles creativity, self-discovery, and the student's unique purpose. That is not education but indoctrination seeded from an internal voice of bigotry.

"The function of education is to teach one to think intensively and to think critically. Intelligence plus character — that is the goal of true education." — Martin Luther King, Jr.

When I was in high school, I thought that I was rebellious. Though I am sure my actions could have been more mature, in retrospect, I recognize that my stubbornness was actually a refusal to be taught not to think. I was determined to think independently and to act according to my personal convictions. In fact, I purposely failed one of my classes over a "principled cause". From my 17-year-old's perspective, the teacher was biased as he made judgments as to why people do what they do, and I considered him judgmental and hypocritical. When given the exams, I would write, "This is the answer you want, but I disagree…" which was followed by my detailed explanation. He marked my answers wrong every time even though I wrote the answer he wanted prior to the reason for my disagreement. Needless to say, I failed the class. Even still, I believed that I achieved something greater. I was proud of myself for not conforming.

I love the up-and-coming generations because I recognize the powerful voices that are theirs intrinsically. I have tolerance for their occasional immature response because I see their potential. They innately carry a treasure — a contribution that could impact society for good! You see, each of us can embrace a perspective of mutual partnership in which *everyone* is able to bring his or her ideas to the collective table. My teacher wanted me to *color within the lines* rather than think outside his ideological box. I was not the only one who disagreed with him. I was, however, the only one willing to risk "failure" by challenging his bias.

Experiential Reality

Everyone has a life story filled with chapters of all kinds. Some are colored with wonderful memorials while others are tattered with hurt and marked with scars. Some of our experiences hold beautiful memories while others bring recollections of injustice and emotional pain. Earlier I wrote about the deep-seated attitudes of gender prejudice that I held inside as a young woman. My man-hating viewpoints stemmed from painful childhood incidents of sexual molestation. Because of the trauma I endured through the acts of certain men, mindsets were established within me that "all men" were evil and out for my harm. My subjective reality triggered years of fear-driven, emotionally charged thoughts and actions. For example, my *women's-libber* line of attack was not driven by equality but dominance as a reaction to my experience. On a positive note, however, those same experiences motivated me to fight against all forms of injustice and any abuse of power. My heart was, and still is, broken for the oppressed and the marginalized. It is not what happens to us, but how we respond to those events that either render us powerless *or* empower us. I have experienced both sides.

Every human being innately carries a valuable contribution to society. He or she possesses a beautiful and unique voice and passion. This distinctive gold will either be released in purity or tainted by a harmful response to one's personal reality. My experiences sourced the young, angry, emotionally wounded man-hater that I was. Today, however, through much healing, the pain of my past is now an instrument in my heart and soul to be a voice of justice on behalf of others.

Society/Culture

Every individual hears the loudest voices of society in his or her culture. They are continually screaming in our ears to conform. It is so easy to agree with the courts of public opinion rather than searching out objective, fact-based truth for ourselves. We often observe that those who scream "prejudice" the loudest are already steeped in their own internal voice of bigotry. We see entire generations shaped by Hollywood, news media, or social networking, none of which are fountains of truth. Even when we are able to recognize that our culture is holding our minds captive, it can be intimidating to explore unfamiliar principled territory. It takes great courage to steward our thoughts objectively.

Life has not been fair for anyone on the planet — past or present. Every person has his or her story of injustice, disappointment, painful circumstances, and prejudicial confrontations from people who are fearful or ignorant. Hearts are broken as horror stories are heard of his or her ancestry or historical accounts of discrimination. Others carry a shattered heart of empathy that compels them to fight for those who are suffering and to be a voice for those who cannot speak for themselves.

Every person must recognize that he or she possesses the power to either accept or reject the negative, fear-based thoughts, attitudes, feelings, and beliefs that knock at his or her mind's door. Opportunities are presented to every person to accept the invitation to be angry, critical, or to pre-judge. We must ask ourselves the question, "Do we want to help our land to heal or do we want to perpetuate a culture of brokenness?" As leaders, it will take great courage and emotional maturity to push beyond our personal emotion-filled, belief-shaping experiences in order for relationships to be restored and our nation mended. Do we want to be proven right or do we want to have value-building relationships?

Are we willing to view every person as an individual and reject the temptation to judge the majority by the minority?

Human beings are profoundly designed neurologically to be self-governing with the innate ability to manage themselves and their resources. That being said, we do not have the legal, moral, or ethical right to control or oppress another. Any attempt to govern a person through fear-based domination is injustice and only forms and reinforces unhealthy, self-sabotaging beliefs and behaviors. Every human being has the power to think, feel, believe, and act in ways that are beneficial for themselves and the common good. When an individual or exclusive spheres of society function in oppression, usury, or devaluation, the proverbial line has been crossed, violating the gift of self-governance.

The very purpose for the laws-of-the-land is to protect the abused from the abuser and bring safety from the exploitation of the oppressor. Leadership is a place of unprejudiced influence; when that power is used to protect the whole — and not only a select group — healing will bubble up as a refreshing fountain for all. When authorized protectors have a heart for the common good, all of society is physically and emotionally safe. However, when the powers that be become the oppressors, injustice flourishes and the people grieve as fear dominates the environment.

As we confront the internal voice of bigotry and become an instrument of justice using our power for good, we will love life and become a part of the solution in a world that so desperately needs us. We can be a catalyst for healthy change when we choose to think positively and act maturely rather than respond through the anger-filled filter of prejudice. Just because someone hates me does not mean I should hate them or be internally manipulated by their actions. I am powerful enough to choose the direction of my inner man.

Healthy Self-Assessment

The more self-aware we are, the better leadership decisions we will make. We will enjoy the internal peace of self-governance and demonstrate authentic validation towards others. It takes courage to ask the hard questions in order to silence the internal voice of bigotry, no matter how small or insignificant it may seem. A small seed-thought of pre-judgment can grow into the largest, deeply rooted belief. You, however, are powerful enough to assess every thought and reject any negative influence within yourself. You can choose to lead with purity of thought and integrity of character.

We must ask ourselves some questions: Am I willing to perform my own internal non-biased investigation, think impartially and objectively, and make fully adult leadership decisions? Do I have the courage to challenge the loudest voices of an agenda-driven culture to serve a higher cause that benefits all of humanity? Am I willing to confront every prejudicial or offensive thought that fights to cross the threshold of my mind? Am I willing to look at different perspectives, listen to another's story, and be a part of their healing journey? Am I willing to say, "I was wrong, forgive me?"

We must have the courage to deal with any internal voice of predisposition and bias. We can be leaders whose voices and methodologies build bridges for healthy dialogue. We can model the way of acceptance, forgiveness, and charity so that relationships and society can be healed.

Healthy leaders must take *the road less traveled;* let us be the ones who travel this road!

CHAPTER THREE
The Internal Voice of Bigotry

Has prejudice escalated or has it only become more visible? Either way, it is harmful. It is scarring for those consumed in its prison and dangerously contagious for those swayed by its display. Many assume the anger associated with corruption and injustice, but sadly direct it in an injurious and divisive way. One fact remains: observable prejudice would never be exhibited if it did not first originate in an internal dialogue.

It is my premise that prejudice has *not* increased. Rather, for a long period it remained quietly seething inside the hearts and minds of those both affected and infected by it. Even at specific times and seasons when things seemed better, calmer, more peaceful without visible eruptions of bigotry, a lack of public attention does not mean that there was not an active *volcano* of prejudice bubbling in the hushed tones of society.

I have traveled to the beautiful nation of Nicaragua more times than I can remember. Nestled in the middle of Central America, Nicaragua is known as the Land of Lakes and Volcanoes, housing 58 volcanoes, six of which are active. I have had the amazing experience of hiking a couple of these lava-housing mountains during my trips there. I was in awe of the beauty of the tropical foliage as I looked at the prettiest orchids that just grow randomly everywhere. Without the awareness that I was hiking an active volcano, it could appear to be the most beautiful paradise. However, there was more to this utopia than met the eye. What I saw on the outside was not a *true* representation of what was below the surface — a fiery-hot burning core.

The raging blaze burning deep within the *heart* of the volcano soon became evident as we moved towards fractures (vents) in the ground where scorching steam and volcanic materials escaped. At this point it became very important to watch where I walked to protect myself from being burned by the steam.

About 25 kilometers from Nicaragua's capital city of Managua, the Masaya Volcano was covered in volcanic ash and rock. As I walked, I felt the heat penetrating through the thick soles of my shoes. It was like walking on a hot oven. The heat was inescapable because the pressure of the core magna reservoir puts constant force to fracture the earth's crust.

As we walked to the top of the volcano, I experienced an intimidating sight as I looked directly into the mouth of the Masaya Volcano. It was like looking into the mouth of hell as boiling liquid fire spewed uncontrollably. It was scorching hot and threatening in its capability to harm. I didn't want to stay in that vulnerable place too long. I realized that at any point that volcano had the potential to release what was in its mouth and cover the landscape with its devastation.

The internal voice of bigotry is like hellfire inside of our minds stoked by our thoughts. It broods and stirs within just waiting to explode and trigger mass devastation that divides people, communities, and nations. Thus my proposition that prejudice has not increased but has been there all along. It has only been waiting for the opportunity to move from the fear-based core of our soul and out of our mouth to bring ruin.

We cannot simply bury or hide the voice of bigotry; we must silence it completely! I think of it like this: if I do not deal with the prejudice that is inside of myself, it will ultimately bring harm to the people who *could have* been my greatest assets, colleagues, and friends. It will steal opportunities for me to enjoy heart connections, and on a broader scale, taint my ability to celebrate and appreciate the nation and people that I love. The fact is that when I choose *not* to embrace diversity, I am sabotaging myself. Our success both individually and together could very well be — and undoubtedly is — through partnerships with those who are completely different than us.

Not Innate but Adapted Beliefs

Former president of South Africa Nelson Mandela courageously stood against apartheid; he said, "No one is born hating another person because of the color of their skin, or his background, or his religion. People must learn to hate, and if they learn to hate, they can be taught to love, for love comes more naturally to the human heart than its opposite[5]".

We are not genetically or innately predisposed towards prejudice. Beginning in the womb, we are being taught and influenced as information enters our five senses in rapid-fire progression. This happens both consciously and subconsciously. When we accept the thoughts associated with that information, neural memory is formed; this is much like data entering a computer. The more we process a thought, the more established the memory is within our mind-brain. This memory creates an automatic pattern of thought or belief that shapes our actions.

The old adage is true that *you reap what you sow*. A farmer could never harvest crops if he or she did not first plant the seed. Some claim that prejudice is spiraling out of control. If that supposition is true, we must be consciously confronting every *seed* planted in our children and youth. As leaders and influencers, we must be personally compelled to raise our voices and courageously stand against the propagation of misinformation and divisiveness.

Science has proven that our brains are wired for love and validation (for more on this topic see my book "Higher Living Leadership"). All we have to do is observe a small child and witness the value they place upon trusted relationships. They have a core need to be loved and they display that love to others — especially other children — without fear. Little human beings have no race, gender, religious, or political bias. They do not care if a person is rich or poor, young or old, highly educated or intellectually challenged. They do, however, have an innate ability to know if they are safe and loved.

Seeds of bias and prejudice begin to limit a child's independent creative thinking; stereotypes become their fear-based knee-jerk reaction. Dr. Jon Lieff, a specialist in neurophysiology says,

> Complex brain circuits are correlated with prejudice and stereotyping. Prejudicial behavior is based on multiple inputs — a rapid amygdala fear response, higher-level slower emotional responses, and conceptual cognitive responses. **All of these are trained, mostly by unconscious social suggestions...**[6]

One day, my oldest grandson was visiting at our house. He has always been an affectionate child and loves to watch movies with his "Mem and Pap." That day we cuddled up in our recliners to watch a true story called "Woodlawn". This movie is set in the early 1970s in Birmingham, Alabama. It depicts a talented, young black football player who is required to face the intense racial tensions and confront the culturally acceptable division and prejudice around him.

At 9 years old, my grandson had never been exposed to blatant racial prejudice. His whole life, he had been positively influenced by loving and trusted individuals of various races. The thoughts of inequality or bias due to race had never crossed his mind because those seeds were never planted there. As the movie began to unfold, he shockingly inquired why these black football players were treated so badly. I shared with him the truth that there were, and still are, narrow-minded prejudiced people in the world. He became quite upset and with great emotion he said repeatedly, "That is wrong! No one should be treated unfairly!" I agreed with him and used this as an opportunity to tell him how to respond to anyone who would speak with bigotry.

He became increasingly emotional and absorbed in this true story as the movie continued. At one point he looked at me and with anger said a *bad* word he was taught not say about anyone: *stupid*. "That is just **stupid**! That is just **stupid**!" I agreed with him and said, "Yes, it is stupid." Racial prejudice had never been seeded into his young mind; therefore, he saw it for what it was and is — **stupid**!

He was also angry. The emotions of anger take place when we feel devalued or shamed. We also feel anger when our convictions are violated. Often we blame anger for behavior, however, the problem is not the emotions of anger, but rather our response to it. That moment was the appropriate time to teach my grandson how to respond to the anger he felt in order to be a voice of justice in a productive way.

Culture has the potential to subconsciously coach us into accepting ways of thinking that are counter-productive for success, healthy relationships, teamwork, and leadership.

My book "Higher Living Leadership" explains:

> Culture is a reproducible system of beliefs that shape the actions of individuals. It communicates to others what are, and are not acceptable beliefs and actions. Culture tells you what is right or wrong and what you must do to "fit in." We learn our culture through instruction and observed behavior.

> Most would agree that we live in a global culture where there is a widespread epidemic of mistrust. Decisions are often stress-filled and fear-driven and the most common mentalities are self-serving and self-gratifying. At the same time, there is a remnant of emerging and established leaders who combat this epidemic by serving as catalysts for positive change in their realms of influence.[7]

My husband and I live in rural Pennsylvania. We moved from the Midwest to a small white German community in 1982. At that time, the area was singularly cultured with no ethnic diversity to be found; nor was it welcomed. I am of German decent and my husband's heritage is English, Scottish, and Irish. We are both as white as white gets, and even we, because we were not born here, were not welcomed. We were told, "You'll never be accepted here so you might as well leave."

My husband grew up in Kansas City, Missouri's inner city, and we met in the D.C. metro area. Both of us have always loved diversity, and we weren't thrilled to have found ourselves in the midst of the monotone countryside. Because we too were "outsiders," not welcomed by the locals, we would often head to the city for a reprieve from *small-town thinking*. Nevertheless, we knew it was where we were supposed to be. Rather than leaving and instead of conforming, we purposed to confront prejudice head on in every way possible. We welcomed our friends of other races to come. As a woman, I caused *an uproar* by taking on roles traditionally reserved for men. Even though the culture said that we didn't belong, we made it our home and were determined to set a countercultural precedent. Today, many years later, the social and racial terrain is vastly different in a beautiful way. The area is welcoming and safe! While small thinking remains among the few — as with anywhere — their voices fall on deaf ears to the majority. Our children grew up here, and now our grandchildren are being raised here as well. They enjoy our picturesque little community!

Our home rests on seven beautiful acres of land. As much as I love it, I recognize that the bigger the acreage, the more labor-intensive it is to manage.

I have found that it is easier to uproot a maple tree seedling than it is to remove a matured tree after 20, 30, or 40 years. At our home, we had a huge, ugly tree at the base of our driveway. It was very much alive, but I hated that tree! It was so big, towering more than 40 feet high. I was faced with two choices: I could have my husband risk life and limb to cut it down or pay a large amount of money to hire a professional. I chose to pay the financial price because of love for my husband. A human being holds much greater value than an ugly seed that grew out of control!

It took four men with all their fancy machinery four hours to cut down that tree. It would have been better if that seedling had never taken root. As leaders, we must manage our internal world with greater fervor. We must shoulder the responsibility to avoid seeding a generation with our painful experiences, fear-based assumptions, and prejudicial mindsets. This is not difficult to do if we first pay the price to silence our own internal narrative of prejudice, as slight as it may be. If we can overcome what was seeded through personal and family experiences or cultural indoctrination, we will speak, influence, and propagate a message that supports healing. We don't have to hide our experiences. We can, however, communicate them with a message that will empower people to be free from mindsets that are destructive to their personal and professional success. We can communicate information without imposing a set of stereotypical beliefs. We can communicate the pain of our past from a position of powerful purpose-filled choices.

When we can confront the internal voice of bigotry through self-awareness, accurate information, and empathetic and honest communication, we can dismantle what divides us, build bridges that cross every prejudicial gap, and heal the wounded heart.

Challenges are a part of life. They authenticate courage and build confidence as we journey through all opposition, whether internal or external. However, fear-based memory will not flourish in the mind of the brave! Instead of stereotyping groups of people, we can look for opportunities to find the good in our fellow man. We can model the way of intrinsic power by making healthy, peace-driven decisions and channeling our reactions to negative world events into powerful and solution-driven responses. This is not the time in history where passive and silent bias remains acceptable or justified in our thoughts or attitudes. Rather than quietly avoiding or suppressing prejudicial "lava" once more, awaiting a repeated eruption, let us be the ones who change the narrative by bringing healing to hearts and lands.

CHAPTER FOUR
Where There is Pride, There is Prejudice

Wherever there is pride, there is prejudice. The inordinate superiority of pride has manifested itself both subtly through stereotypes, bias, and assumptions *and* overtly through blatant acts of vile injustices. History cannot record the enormity of this man-made epidemic. However, it has painfully influenced generation after generation. Pride, prejudice, and injustice are abuses of power — injustices as old as humanity. Pride generates a mindset of devaluation to anyone or anything that does not meet its inflated standards. It is the bedrock to the arrogance of supremacy.

Every type of supremacy is nauseatingly evil. For example, white supremacy is a radical ideology that promotes the belief that *whites* are the superior race and should dominate other races. It has been evident throughout history — 400 years of the trans-Atlantic slave trade, neo-Nazism, the South African apartheid, and the American Jim Crow laws that enforced racial segregation — just to name a few. Disappointingly, there are individuals who continue to hold this destructive belief. It provides them with a faulty internal vindication to commit acts of injustice against others, whether privately or publicly.

Simply, anyone who adopts a supremacy mindset of any kind has become an instrument to propagate injustice in our communities and nations. Someone with this mindset often carries an air of self-ascribed self-importance. Behind this veil of superiority is almost always found underlying issues of one's own shame and fear. Hatred toward anyone different than oneself reveals internal insecurity and powerlessness. You see, the fear-based actions of pride and prejudice are often internally driven by weakness, the very opposite of what is being outwardly portrayed. "Hatred of others can only exist in a person who secretly hates themselves."[8]

In order to silence prejudgment, we must assess the thoughts and voices of bigotry that we entertain internally. If we desire our external world to change, we must first transform our internal world. To judge my internal beliefs in leniency and judge my external world harshly is hypocritical. As I write in my book, "Higher Living Leadership",

> I will subconsciously create an atmosphere that mirrors what is taking place on the inside of me — I can only conceal my private perspectives and perceptions for the short term...

> Any internal perceptions will eventually leak out, especially when pressure is applied. We will "disturb the peace" externally if we do not possess internal peace. If I am consistently discontented with life, I will create crisis and drama externally. Anger, fear, frustration, negativity, and dissatisfaction will seep out, affecting the atmosphere and others.[9]

I used the example of white supremacy, but the fact of the matter is that anyone can choose to walk in this prideful act of prejudice.

Religious Pride and Prejudice

The Crusades from 1095 to 1291 demonstrated blatant prejudice as both Christians and Muslims pursued the extermination of the opposing religion through blood violence. These were dark times and totally contradictory to the true nature of a loving God. Now, hundreds of years later, we receive reports of ISIS (Islamic State in Iraq and Syria) that broadcast the torture and/or murder of anyone who disagrees or opposes their beliefs. "They are absolutely killing every Christian they see ... This is absolutely genocide in every sense of the word. They want everyone to convert, and they want sharia law to be the law of the land."[10] ISIS's hatred is seeded into

every aspect of their culture. Their children are being indoctrinated but also recruited to fight and even die for their unjust cause.

As another example, let's look at Germany during the Third Reich period. Those of the Jewish faith did not have the same rights as other citizens. Jewish citizens were prevented from pursing certain vocations and holding positions of prominence. Anti-Semitic Nazi Germany's goal was the extermination of the Jewish race as well as their religion. As a result, over 6 million Jews were murdered, along with many Jehovah's Witnesses.

Religious prejudice is a present-day reality for so many. Pew Research Center reports on the rising tide of restrictions on religion through legislation banning or limiting religious expression within organizations and private citizens globally[11]. Social intimidations are evidenced through harassment, violence, criminality, and even death.

Religious pride and prejudice is not always overt but gives preferential treatment towards the preferred religious belief and limits the freedoms of others.

Racial Pride and Prejudice

The perpetrators behind the Holocaust targeted individuals for more than just religion. It was one of the most strategic and systematic plans and the poster child for white supremacy. Adolf Hitler's Nazi Germany purposed to exterminate all those who were not of the Aryan "master race." In addition to the 6 million Jewish people who were murdered, Romani (gypsy), Polish, homosexuals, those of Slavic or African ethnicity, physically or mentally disabled, and many more were targeted as well. This was the genocide of approximately 11 million people. I cannot *wrap my head around* the degenerate mindset that would give license to such an atrocity. It is horrific!

What allowed the Germany citizenry to accept the actions of their government as millions were displaced, enslaved, or murdered? The deliberate prideful indoctrination of the masses began as hatred was publicized. Different races were considered inferior and therefore devalued, no longer considered human.

As I mention in "Higher Living Leadership", "This same strategy took place in slave-states, giving slave owners the right to treat 'their property' in any way they deemed beneficial for them. For the most part, the treatment of those of African descent in the United States was inhumane, cruel, and devaluing.[12]"

"Slaves were punished by whipping, shackling, hanging, beating, burning, mutilation, branding, and/or imprisonment ... Pregnant women received the most horrendous lashings; slave masters came up with unique ways to lash them so that they could beat the mother without harming the baby. Slave masters would dig a hole big enough for the woman's stomach to lay in and proceed with the lashing."[13]

The South African apartheid laws divided the racial groups as they lived and grew separately. They could not integrate socially and intermarriage was prohibited. The result was an advantaged minority verses the disadvantaged majority. One race was deemed superior while the others inferior, which is foundational to all forms of racial pride and prejudice.

The sad reality is that today racial prejudice continues to be a painful experience for far too many. I will unpack this more in future chapters. It's time for a paradigm shift!

Political Pride and Prejudice

When political agendas become seedbeds for abuses of power, it is destructive to a nation and the people it is commissioned to serve. When a nation's citizenry is manipulated to obtain a political platform rather than using these platforms of power for the good of the people, we see the devastation.

A contemporary example is evidenced in Venezuela. Former president Hugo Chavez came into power proclaiming to fight against corruption only to unleash greater widespread exploitation of the people. After Hugo's death, President Nicolas Maduro was elected from the United Socialists Party of Venezuela. The Venezuelan people have rapidly lost their rights through intimidation, censorship, and prosecution. The nation is in chaos.

I have given much thought to political pride and prejudice. Wrestling over power and agendas rather than focusing on healing can position a nation to implode under the weight of bigotry. This is a *volcano* that we do not want to erupt!

Ethnic Pride and Prejudice

On one of my visits to Kenya, East Africa, I met the most beautiful young woman living in Nairobi. Her name is Frida. She was young, tall, elegant, and astonishingly gorgeous. Her demeanor was confidently gentle as she carried herself with the refinement of a wealthy diplomat's daughter. Our conversation rapidly moved from a casual inquiry of her greatest passion to the heart-wrenching story of her life. It was a story of politically generated tribal hatred and prejudice with those of the same race. As she shared, I learned that she was a victim of the Rwandan genocide that began in 1994. During that time, over 800,000 people of the minority Tutsi tribe were killed by the rival majority Hutu tribe.

At a mere 14 years old, Frida found herself crouched in horror next to her family members inside the only home she ever knew. They heard the screams of their neighbors as the Hutu tribe systematically moved from house to house, slaughtering her family's Tutsi friends and neighbors. Somehow making matters even worse was the surreal awareness that those killing their loved ones were also their fellow villagers; they didn't come from a distant land to carelessly slaughter strangers. Rather, these were the same people they had played with and gone to school with as children; they ate at each other's homes. Before this genocide began, they were friends. Now there was nowhere to run, no way to escape, so they held each other for the last time helplessly waiting for their executioners to come.

When their Hutu neighbors arrived, they brutally raped and violently beat Frida, her sisters, and mother. Frida watched as they decapitated her mother next to her. With violent ferocity, a bloodbath ensued. Frida, along with 15 of her family members, were buried in a single large mass grave piled on top of each other. They covered the grave with stones, branches, and leaves. Their Hutu killers thought that all were dead. Unbeknownst to them, beneath the ground, the unconscious Frida's heart was still beating.

Frida came to consciousness in the middle of the night. She was paralyzed from the waist down, but she somehow managed to pull herself out of the grave, inch by inch. She dragged herself into the woods using only her arms, searching for a place to hide. There are many more details to Frida's story, but alas, she made her way to a refugee camp and was sent to Kenya for safety and recovery.

Recalling our conversation from many years ago, I continue to experience a dichotomy of emotions as I did that day. My heart was broken. I was furious as a whirlwind of thoughts raged inside of me. But at the same time, I was overwhelmed with the grace that Frida still managed to carry. Not many years after these events took place, she shared how she willingly returned to the same Hutu tribe members who viciously murdered her family and left her for dead. She forgave them. Her incredible story of forgiveness for those who slaughtered those she loved was and is truly remarkable. Her extraordinary journey from brokenness to wholeness affected my heart deeply all those years ago and still does today.[14]

The beautiful young woman I met that day in Kenya refused pride, prejudice, and all the ugly things that accompany it. No one could ever blame her if she were angry, bitter, and wanted revenge, but instead she choose a *road less traveled*. Her brave choices positioned her for a life to love and the ability to influence countless others. I will never forget Frida, her story, or the personal power she possessed to rise above the horror she experienced.

Frida's story brings to light the powerful influence of politics and ethnicity to devastate lives, communities, and even nations. Friends had become enemies as they were incited by a government ruled by Hutu power. Could it even be possible that a political agenda could drive a mass genocide? It did! Could a political divide separate lifelong trusted relationships? It did! Is it plausible that people could demonstrate more loyalty to a political ideology than to valuable human beings? It happened — not so long ago. It is a frightening thought to see the pervasive ability that pride and prejudice has upon the passive mind that believes the loudest and most prevalent voice.

> *Without clearly knowing our identity and purpose, we will find ourselves echoing the loudest voice we hear!*

Gender Pride and Prejudice

Whether male chauvinists or man-hating women, both are destructive to emotional health, mature relationships, a safe home environment, and the widespread impact on society.

On a trip to Portugal, my husband and I stumbled upon male-dominated *pride and prejudice* concerning women. It was not blatant abuse; however, there was a definite air of superiority in the men's interaction with women. My husband Steven's shrewd response to this sexist culture touched my heart not only as his wife, but also as a representative of womankind. He had an opportunity to speak to this particular group and asked them a question, "How many of you would like half of your body paralyzed?" All responded with a resounding "no!" They didn't grasp why he was asking this. Steven began to convey that when women are confined within a prejudicial box, half of the population is metaphorically paralyzed; this hinders our ability to make progress and advance as a whole. These men soon discovered their *internal voice of bigotry*. When we limit others, it sabotages our unified potential.

I have traveled to a nation where patriarchal authority gave the man the right to have sexual relationships with any female who lived under his roof. This was culturally acceptable! When girls entered puberty, they underwent the horrific practice of female genital mutilation. The effects of these accepted practices resulted in these precious young girls living in the wake of emotional and physical shame. They could not see their beauty, value, or worth. My heart was breaking! After a few years of building trusted relationships with the people of this nation, the leadership provided me with the honor of speaking into their lives. With great sensitivity, I addressed these culturally destructive traditions. The men were incredibly humble as the *internal voice of bigotry* was confronted with medical facts and a message of value on behalf of the women. Their eyes filled with tears, but more importantly, their hearts were softened at the stark realization of what they previously had not considered. That day, at least for those present, the culture began to change in their homes.

> *It is impossible to control someone's heart or legislate their convictions, but we can be a voice of truth, justice, and reconciliation.*

In different places all over our world it is culturally acceptable to devalue women and to treat them as property. In some nations, honor killings are practiced when a woman has brought *dishonor* to their family, even for the smallest infraction; she is blamed when victimized through rape. She puts her life in danger for desiring a divorce from an abusive husband. Young girls are sold or forced into marriage propagated from poverty, tradition, or simply gender prejudice.

Looking in our own back yard I've witnessed forward movement from my "woman's liberation" days. However, the fact remains that women are still the dominant target for sex crimes, continue to fight for equal pay for equivalent positions, and are often relegated to stereotypical family roles.

Every woman deserves to be free from violence and male domination. Her marriage should be a place of safety, never something to cause her to live as a *slave* in her own home. Many girls are disallowed education, and many women are denied the right to vote or the ability to earn a fair wage, and are demoralized sexually.

When cultural events are propagated generationally and become socially expedient, the conscious mind adapts. The man shields himself from any sense of guilt from his violent and cruel attitudes and actions towards women. The man's cultural reality accepts that it is morally right and true that his responsibility is to control the lesser sex. The woman's ability to discover her humanity and sense of value ceases to exist. Her response often becomes fear-driven compliancy.

Gender prejudice is also subtly woven into culture and often ambiguous in both personal and professional interaction. When we must justify our degrading comments with a defensive response, covering it up as a "joke" or brushing it under the rug as if it had no effect, our biased point of view will become known. Whenever gender is viewed through a filter of pride — seeing one as greater than another — it will always divide rather than unite. This pride will justify our right to overvalue our worth and undervalue another's, which perpetuates competition rather than collaboration. However, when we can see each other as equals in value, each with something to contribute that the other needs, we can finally embrace our full collective potential.

Generational Pride and Prejudice

There are five generations that occupy our modern-day society. Each has unique experiences that have shaped their thoughts, beliefs, and actions. For any generation, it can be challenging to relate to the perceptions and perspectives of a different age group. I have chosen to focus my attention on the generational prejudices and stereotypes that apply to the United States; however, every nation has their own generational differences and stereotypes.

The Traditionalists/Silent generation born before 1945 lived in a completely different world than the Millennials born after 1980 or the Gen Z/ Centennials born after 2000.

Many times in honoring our personal history, we demonstrate an attitude of superiority towards another generation. We may inadvertently construct prejudicial mindsets and bias simply because we think differently than those who have lived longer or shorter than us. The consequences of this can cause us to develop stereotypes that hinder our capacity to value one another and sabotage our ability to partner together effectively.

Stereotypical labeling is destructive. No human being is the same, even if born in the same generation. Yes, there are certain strengths or potential weaknesses that can be connected to an age group; however, every individual has the ability to walk out his or her unique identity and purpose and release an irreplaceable contribution to society.

It is inherently wrong to spew judgments condemning another for your own failure to relate or understand.

Generational Stereotypes

Let's look at some general stereotypes connected to the five living generations at the time of this writing. (Please note that birth years are general timeframes and sources differ slightly because of characterizations in different parts of the world.)

Traditionalist/Silent Generation (born before 1945): Behind the times and no longer effective or influential in the advancement of our present-day society. They are practical, value hard work, and follow rules dutifully.

Baby Boomers (born 1946 to 1965): At the time of this writing, they make up one-quarter of the population. They are seen as "out of touch" but do not want to leave the workforce. They are ignorant of technology and are workaholics.

Generation X (born 1966 to 1979): At this time in history, they are the most productive workforce, but are labeled as independent, skeptical, cynical, and distrustful.

Millennials/Generation Y (born 1980 to 2000): Valued for their technological ability and big vision, they are considered lazy, entitled, and are non-conformists.

Centennials/Generation Z (born after 2000): Labeled as indolent and unprepared for the workforce while also being the biggest consumers.

Validation Dismantles Stereotypes

When we value someone we will protect them, treat them as valuable, sacrifice for them, and invest into them. In addition, our value of a person or persons allows us to unequivocally partner with them. Partnership is a two-way street with both sides committed to honoring and being honorable. The stereotypes listed above do the opposite; rather than encouraging partnership, they divide and provoke the devaluation of treasured individuals who have the ability to positively impact their world for good.

Do you realize that it was the Silent Generation who paid the price to build the institutions that benefit the world today? We should be so grateful that they continue to put others' needs above their own. When my mother (born 1923) was in her 80s, she was determined to stay connected with her children and grandchildren. Having never typed a day in her life, she purchased the newest and best computer on the market and learned how to use it. Now in her 90s, she has since upgraded her computer and uses the internet to shop for bargains and communicate with her kids, grandkids, and great-grandkids on social media. In addition, she still visits shut-ins and nursing homes to show value to those who have been marginalized.

The Baby Boomers — one of whom I am — do not necessarily live by a 40-hour workweek. I find great fulfillment in my work and enjoy impacting society for good. This generation includes many of our corporate leaders and the ones who pushed through societal injustices to pave the way for the generations to follow.

As aforementioned, Generation X is the most productive generation in today's workforce. They are the first generation to actively engage in technology, have an entrepreneurial mindset, and carry the balance of leadership abilities and the motivation to make their world a better place.

As I write this, Millennials are getting the most attention in our media. I personally do not remember corporate workshops training leaders how to understand, motivate, and manage a generation. Millennials are passionate, visionary, and driven by social justice. They have moved away from the big house, big car success model to beg the question: *what is really important?* They aspire to live full lives, cultivate meaningful relationships, and to make their world a better place.

The fact is that every generation is unfairly labeled by its predecessors. However, this narrative begins to change as both the former and the latter groups grow older and mature, and their accomplishments are placed within perspective as their societal contributions are actualized and appreciated.

This leads to the current youngest living generation — the Centennials — who were literally born at the turn of a new century. It's amazing how one generation will learn from its forerunners. Centennials are less idealistic and more pragmatic. They are more content with clothes from a vintage store than having the designer label. They are solution-driven, focused on resiliency, and have a desire to be trustworthy and authentic.

If we are going to be influential leaders, we must embrace mutually empowering partnerships that connect the generations. By choosing to focus on the best of each generation, we will gain the proliferating ability to be better together than we could ever be on our own. We must extinguish generational pride and prejudice so that we do not isolate ourselves and sabotage our endeavors to impact our world for good.

Pride and prejudice is found in the hearts of the rich *and* the poor, the executives *and* the subordinate, in political and ideological differences, urban versus rural communities, and the list can go on and on.

We cannot allow our past experiences or present circumstances to define who we are today, determine where we are going, or limit what we can achieve. Likewise, we must not permit prejudice to hinder our ability to partner with others, even if they are different than us or have their own perspective.

In our multi-dimensional lives, we will experience good and bad days all in the same day. We may find that pain and purpose often border one another and that hope and disappointment run a close race. This dichotomy is a part of life. Therefore, if we can learn to avoid negative thoughts and permanent decisions in the midst of temporary emotions, we will find peace *without* pre-judgment. We will position ourselves despite the battles that we face in this world and become a part of the solution.

Conclusion

This chapter is painted with a principled broad stroke. An entire book could be written for each topic, and there are many other practices and beliefs of pride and prejudice. The key is to recognize the many faces of pride, supremacy, and pre-judgment in our own lives so we can take personal responsibility for *our* thoughts. It is also important for us, as leaders of influence, to determine our course of action to be a voice of hope, a generator of validation, and an instrument of justice.

"The ultimate measure of a man is not where he stands in moments of comfort and convenience, but where he stands at times of challenge and controversy."
— Martin Luther King, Jr.

CHAPTER FIVE
Prejudice Propagates Injustice

All over our world, justice-minded individuals are raising their voices and investing their lives and resources to aid those in the grips of injustice. Countless not-for-profit organizations have, and continue to be, established with the sole purpose of serving their fellowman. These individuals are societal heroes because every act of compassion helps to heal our land. When we hold justice as an intrinsic core value, our lives and leadership become a catalyst for positive change; we become hands of aid and solution providers for the world's most heart-wrenching sufferings. I write in my book Higher Living Leadership,

> Justice has to do with the exercise and distribution of power, authority, influence, and wealth. This power is visible in the political and governmental arenas; in social, religious, cultural, family, and educational systems; and in the marketplace. When we use this power to do what is good we become an instrument of justice. But, when power is used to take from others what is rightfully theirs, injustice results. Today, we are witnessing blatant evil that saturates cultures with lies, hatred, and injustice and strategically plans to destroy anyone who believes differently.[15]

Injustice is an abuse of power that is propagated through prejudice. You can never devalue, abuse, be critical of, or commit acts of injustice towards anyone without some form of pre-judgment, discrimination, mindsets of supremacy, or bigotry.

As we looked at the arrogance of Adolf Hitler, we realized he could not have abused his power without prejudice and his message of dehumanization. Perverted ideologies were the foundation that gave license to exterminate millions. In fact, his extreme prejudice was a voice that saturated the Nazi regime and the entire nation. Many who secretly hated his ideologies were bound in fear and held captive in a voiceless prison.

Once again, terrorism such as that performed by the radical Islamic State (ISIS or ISIL) justifies kidnapping, raping, executing, massacring, and striking fear into the masses as they shout, "Death to infidels." Why would they do this? Hatred and prejudicial indoctrination from childhood rule their thoughts and corrupt their actions. Their conscience has become so seared that they no longer see value in anyone who believes differently.

Throughout recorded history, we read accounts of injurious attitudes and injustices carried out without any backlash or consequence to the perpetrator. Past and present-day slavery was, and is, fundamentally driven through prejudice. Who is seen as less than human? Who can be abused without penalty in order to satisfy greed? Who is less valuable and can become forcibly subservient in order to generate profit? Whether it is lust for power, position, reputation, or economic avarice, injustice is the result of these damaging beliefs.

I believe each person has the freedom to make choices for their own lives, but when their freedom takes away another's, it is inherently wrong and an act of injustice.

One thing I love about my nation — the United States of America — is our Constitution,[16] but also the Bills of Rights, which are the first 10 amendments added to the Constitution to protect the people from the abuse of governmental corruption. The government's purpose is to use its power for the good of all its citizenry, serving as an instrument of justice. I celebrate our freedom of speech, religion, right to bear arms, and so forth. However, we cannot overlook our fellow public's *human rights* that allow their fundamental freedom. The belief that all men are created equal allows everyone the opportunity to pursue equal treatment under the law and equal opportunities in our economic system. This is what causes a nation to prosper!

> *If fighting for my rights takes away another's, I become the abuser! Genuine care for another ultimately brings me freedom.*

The 13th amendment was passed in 1865 after our nation faced a brutal civil war and 90 years of slavery. Every person now had the freedom not to be held as a slave, to be bought or sold, or be treated as property. Thank God for that legislation! This added amendment, along with justice-driven abolitionists and courageous individuals like Dr. Martin Luther King, Jr., helped to bring our nation closer to equality. However, the sad commentary is that 150 years later, we see a rise of human trafficking, which aids the institution of modern-day slavery in the form of child labor, sweat shops, sex trafficking, and forced marriages, among others. There are also countless instances of abuses of power, riots, hatred, and prejudice that continue to permeate our world.

> *Having a firm conviction of truth, and protecting the freedom that comes from that truth, is the mandate and essential work of each generation.*

We find similar constitutions and legislation in nations worldwide. While laws of the land can be created and enforced, this alone does not address the central issue of *the internal voice of bigotry.* The core of a man cannot be legislated by anyone but his- or herself. People may outwardly and obligatorily obey the law to protect themselves, but inwardly they are like an active *volcano* ready to erupt when provoked. It is only through confronting our own internal ignorance and fear that we are able to change.

Benjamin Watson, tight end for the New Orleans Saints writes,

> … ultimately the problem is not a SKIN problem, it is a SIN problem. SIN is the reason we rebel against authority. SIN is the reason we

abuse our authority. SIN is the reason we are racist, prejudiced, and lie to cover for our own. SIN is the reason we riot, loot, and burn.[17]

Sin can be defined as a willful choice and intentional violation of an upright and trustworthy principle, standard, or moral code — in other words, an attitude or action that is wicked, immoral or simply wrong.

> *Those who say there are no absolutes are absolutely wrong!*

Sin is birthed from an iniquitous internal dialogue supported by our experience or what we've been taught. Prejudice, assumption, and fear-based bias are emotionally damaging to every person in its wake of sorrow, even the offender.

In the early 1800s, a young man redefined sin in order to challenge the masses to fight for social reformation. I wrote about him in my book, Higher Living Leadership:

> Charles Finney, also known as the Father of Modern Revivalism, was a leader in the Second Great Awakening in the United States. This revival not only impacted the Christian community but was a strong voice of social reformation as he influenced many to confront the atrocities of slavery and other social issues of that day.[18]

Finney said, "I had made up my mind on the question of slavery, and was exceedingly anxious to arouse public attention to the subject ... I so often alluded to slavery, and denounced it, that a considerable excitement came to exist among the people."[19] This young abolitionist helped to define sin for what it was, the destruction, devaluation, and dehumanizing of a human being.

Years ago, I started a foundation called the Voice of Justice Foundation in order to be a voice of hope, the hands of rescue, and an instrument of justice on behalf of the neglected, abused, or shamed. When I ponder the injustice of human trafficking, I see the most economically lucrative greediness in our world reaching over $32 billion annually. The cruelty and brutality of modern slavery is the embodiment of sin.

Abuse of Power

Prejudice in all its forms propagates injustice — the abuse of power! Power is embodied in every form of authority and leadership responsibility. It could be a parent or guardian, educator, governmental leader, employer, spiritual leader, performer, or even the news media. When a platform of influence is prejudiced in any way, it can lead to an abuse of power.

Abuse of power is evidenced when individuals use their influence to benefit themselves at the expense of another.

Here are some examples of abuses of power:

- A schoolteacher showing partiality to the son or daughter of a faculty member;

- A university professor teaching to promote his or her personal agenda or ideologies rather than encouraging independent creative thinking;

- Government officials enacting legislation to further their political career at the expense of the people they are commissioned to serve.

Abuse of power is evidenced in as many different ways as there are people on the planet. It begins in the poisoned and corrupt motives of the abuser. Some actions may appear crueler than others, but to the one being taken advantage of, it is hurtful, conflict-ridden, and unjust. Here are some examples of injustices:

- Gossiping in order to degrade someone else and make oneself emerge superior;

- A salesman embellishing or communicating partial truths in order to make a sale;

- A spouse or parent using anger to manipulate the choices of another;

- Threats of harm to command submission;

- Posing as a friend to a child or his or her family to groom the child for sexual abuse or child prostitution;

- A religious leader abusing, molesting, or manipulating people to satisfy his or her wants or perverted desires;

- A seducer who appears kind, safe, or romantic to lure someone into human trafficking;

- When an employer makes decisions that are injurious to those whom they have hired;

- An employee who steals from the company through substandard work, misusing company time or money or embezzlement;

- Elite personalities, celebrities, or sport figures who use their platform to divide rather than unite or attack rather than heal.

It is fitting for us to remember that the greater the platform of influence, the greater the opportunity to either positively impact humanity or manipulate for personal gain. The famous are positioned with a public visibility that makes them appear credible to the general populace — whether that is true or only an illusion. For personalities who are presented with this honored platform, it behooves them to be voices of justice and to use their power for good.

The more prominent the platform, the greater responsibility is needed to practice wisdom and care for all. The louder our public voice, the more we must live and lead authentically in both our public and private lives, loving deeply from the heart and without prejudice.

CHAPTER SIX
Ignorance — Shame — Fear — Mistrust

Living in an agricultural community, we recognize that crops do not grow in grocery stores. We enjoy the little roadside stands where farmers or enthusiastic gardeners sell their produce. No matter how skilled and ardent the farmers are, they are mindful of the important necessities of the seed, soil, and weather conditions. Their hope is for a bumper crop that allows consumer prices to decrease while their sales and profits increase. Where I live, it is not uncommon to find the locals advertising FREE produce. Friends and neighbors often look to give their excess of cucumbers, tomatoes, corn, or zucchini to anyone who values their harvest.

When there is abundance, every person who so desires can fill his or her belly with nutritious produce. What is even more valuable and surpasses a full belly, however, is the celebration of a healthy community where the people's needs are met. Anyone willing to invest into the community can receive its benefits. But, what happens when the soil is void of nutrients, the seed is genetically modified, and there is a drought in the land? The farmer must work so much harder to water and fertilize to try and make up for the natural deficit. Yet, with all the extra work, the harvest is inadequate and void of nutritional benefits while the prices increase, and needs are not met. People get angry at the cost of produce and complain about its lack of flavor. They proceed to the junk food aisle to fill their stomachs and become addicted to what is bad for them.

Now allow me to use this agricultural example to show you the effects of prejudice. Where it exists, it is a source of barrenness; it breeds an inability to love life, leaves needs unmet, and propels a perpetual cycle of disappointment, frustration, and anger.

The farmer represents every valuable human being who carries the innate desire to succeed.

The seed is the potential that every person has, intrinsically and organically.

The soil simulates the condition of our internal world — our emotional health and thought-life.

The weather conditions portray an individual's unique experiential reality and cultural programming.

Finally, the harvest shows the outcome and consequences of a person's life conceived from their internal voice and external responses.

Instinctively, children are born knowing that their needs were to be met by loving and trustworthy parents. Newborns feel they are a part of their mother well beyond his/her first birthday, and his/her need for the father's investment is insatiable throughout their young lives. They are born with an empty love tank that needs to be filled. When parents and other trusted primary relationships pour into this love tank, the child's physical needs are met; they experience safety, and there is no fear of abandonment. This allows them the ability to begin to learn to trust. The *seed* — their internal world — is bursting with optimism, self-confidence, and an awareness of their potential. They have no doubt that they have *superhero* abilities inside imagining they can do anything.

It is heartbreaking when a child's experiential reality and cultural programming is unfavorable. Their external world forced its way into their bubble of safety. The investments into their *love tank* dwindled, traumatizing them and arresting their ability to come to the fullness of emotional maturity. Their ability to trust is shattered and their needs forsaken.

What happens to the potential? What internal dialogue follows? What do their homes look like when they become the parents? Is it possible for an empty cup to meet the need of another? Or do they exist only to satisfy self at the expense of others — even their children? Is their pursuit to meet their own need so unquenchable that they spend the rest of their lives trusting no one, blaming others, making excuses, and controlling by way of passive or aggressive anger?

Their internal dialogue, actions, and reactions are negative and debilitating. Is it possible to be successful in the eyes of others while our inner voice is screaming, "I just want to love and be loved," "I just want peace," "I just want to know that I matter."

The subsequent harvests are riddled with ignorance, shame, fear, and mistrust which each generate all types of prejudice.

Weather Conditions Affect the Harvest

None of these thoughts and emotions were foreign to me due to the sexual molestation I experienced starting at 2 years old. Our experiential reality is an invitation for the development of our internal self-view and our worldview.

I want to share with you a couple of personal experiences that developed a prejudicial anger in me (a white woman) towards white men.

First and foremost were the repeated sexual violations from the time I was 2 years old to 9 years old — all from white boys or men. Then, immediately upon graduation from high school, I traveled to Kansas City, Missouri — 1,500 miles away from home — to attend an airline personnel resident program. Soon after I got there, I went to a party. I was a hurting young woman and alcohol made me feel brave. I got so drunk that night that I lost all intuitive sense of self-preservation.

There was a group of white guys about my age that decided I was a prime target to gang rape. As they began to aggressively move toward me, a strong, barrel-chested black man in the room intervened. He was my superhero! He was an instrument of justice for this little five-foot-tall white girl. He not only protected me from defilement at that moment, but he took me back to my dorm room and stayed with me until I woke up the next morning. He was genuinely kind, assertively protective, and displayed a purity that amazed me. He became my own personal bodyguard for the rest of my time in Kansas City. I never saw him again after returning to the East Coast, but what he did for me will forever be etched into my memory. I am forever grateful for him!

Because of my experiences, after that time, I decided that it was only safe to date black men. Likewise, if I would ever get married, I wanted to marry a black man. Remembering my grandmother's stellar answer to my race-driven marriage question, my newly discovered conviction was affirmed.

I later learned that character has nothing to do with skin color or ethnicity. I identified with the cry of Dr. Martin Luther King, Jr. when he dreamt of a day when men and women would not be judged by the color of their skin, but by the content of their character.[20]

We are never able to know or appreciate individuals until we take the time to see their hearts and discover what manner of man or woman that they are. What do they say or do when under pressure? How do they treat someone who cannot help them? Will they do the right thing when it is not popular?

My story illustrates that prejudice is shaped by our experiential reality and/ or societal influence. I never consciously processed that emotional sexual imprinting + color of skin + gender = prejudice. These realities were established subconsciously through ignorance, shame, fear, and mistrust.

Ignorance: My personal truth was subjective. There is not one medical or scientific fact that supports that the color of a man's skin reveals their character, integrity, or trustworthiness. I defined truth through my personal pain and I was blind to any other viewpoint.

Shame: My greatest challenge was my inability to see my personal value. Shame produces a false identity causing us to see ourselves through a distorted lens. I believed that I was damaged goods and without value. What did I do wrong that I was molested? Something is terribly wrong with me or this would never have happened to me! The beauty of my self-worth and sense of femininity, as a child and a young adult, was sacrificed on the altar of the selfish violation of the perversion from men.

Fear: Fear is a false reality sustained by real experiences and anticipated threats. I expected to be victimized and, therefore, I subconsciously positioned myself for injustice.

Mistrust: How could I trust someone to come through for me when I could not trust myself? I feared abandonment because my experience screamed to my value that I was damaged and faulty. Without trust, it is impossible to form healthy intimate relationships. Though I was an *alpha* woman in personality, aggressively pursuing success, I was internally driven by the fear of being taken advantage of. I assumed that everyone was a threat, an enemy, a rival, an obstruction to my success story.

The powerful and freeing truth is that we can choose to confront the lies of shame and fear. Without pre-judgment, we can choose a journey of honest, objective discovery and learn to build trust again — one person at a time, recognizing who is or is not worthy of our trust. I know this because I lived it.

These internal tug-of-wars and cycles of emotionally driven assumptions about others and ourselves must stop. It must be understood that every person has a choice to either live by default or by design. I can choose to be controlled by external circumstances or motivated by my innate potential. I have the power to choose to either believe the loudest voices around me or to search for objective truth. Will I believe that I am a powerless victim or a powerful victor? This is my choice! Every person has the same choice.

If we are unable to do this on our own, it is worth it to get help from healthy individuals or professional counselors. We may need assistance in shifting our habits from powerless, subjective reactions to powerful, objective responses. This change, however, will lead to life-transforming freedom not only for you, but also for the world we live in.

What we don't often realize is that every person on the planet from every nation, culture, or race is more alike than different. Man or woman, young or old, rich or poor, executive or new hire, urbanite or country folk, we all have the same core needs, and we all deal with many of the same struggles.

Science speaks to our sameness in the midst of our differences:

> Our DNA provides a unique set of instructions that build us as individuals, however: 'All humans are 99.9 percent identical [in their DNA sequence]...'[21]

An old proverb says, "Treat others in the same way you want to be treated."[22] It turns out we are more like others than we thought.

CHAPTER SEVEN
The Personal Painful Stories of Prejudice

Some may believe that I write out of idealistic sentimentalism in confronting the destructive power of prejudice. Yes, my heart breaks for those who suffer in the wake of injustice, but science informs us what happens neurologically when our thoughts are toxic. I made this same claim in "Higher Living Leadership":

> According to neuroscientists, every thought that we have is either fear- or faith-based, destructive or building, toxic or healthy. Because of the intense emotional component of negative thoughts, they become at least three times more forceful than the positive thoughts.[23]

However, these negative thoughts are not more powerful than the power of personal choice. The objective of maturity is to feed faith-based thoughts (healthy thoughts that build healthy memory) and starve thoughts that are fear-based (destructive thoughts that build unhealthy memory). Part of the process of the brain's maturation is to make neural connections from the reward center — the place of emotional reaction — of the brain to the executive pre-frontal cortex. It is the utilization of the pre-frontal cortex that gives the ability to focus, organize, and strategize. This powerful part of the brain also allows us to make wise decisions separate from emotional reactions, to control impulses, and to assess our thoughts and emotions in order to determine our course of action.

Simply speaking, the thoughts we choose to accept or reject will allow us to think objectively, rather than subjectively, through emotion or experience. This is how we can live in a world filled with difficulties and still love life. This is how we can reject a culture of pride and prejudice.

All prejudice, assumption, bias, and gossip is destructive and toxic to our mind-brain. Negative thoughts are more forceful because they are accompanied by intense emotion, which establishes an automatic fear-based pattern of thought. Though we are not born with prejudice, our minds can quickly adopt belief systems that reject anything that is different than our passion-driven programming. We will fight for a subjective cause, even when faced with objective proof of its inaccuracies because we feel it so strongly and so deeply.

It is human nature to be critical of what we do not understand. Many choose to camp on the dirty banks of disapproval and faultfinding rather than risk getting in the waters of understanding, empathy, compassion, and care for others. We can be washed internally by a choice to hear another's story and learn to love.

The wise Maya Angelo said, "If we lose love and self-respect for each other, this is how we finally die."[24]

Dr. Martin Luther King, Jr. said, "I have decided to stick with love. Hate is too great a burden to bear."[25]

Each one of us have stories of injustice, pain, loss, and sorrow. We can both empathize and be a part of the solution by the way we live, love, and lead, or we can pity ourselves into powerlessness and victimization. Maya Angelo also said, "History, despite its wrenching pain, cannot be unlived, but if faced with courage, need not be lived again."[26]

While writing this book, I asked a large and diverse group of people if they would be so brave as to share their stories with me — and you. I was in awe of the number of responses I received. Many have requested pseudonyms to protect the innocent but wanted to share their past and present battles in order to confront the evil of prejudice personally and head on. I applaud their courage and heart to be a part of the solution!

Allow your heart to feel their pain. How do your experiences connect to theirs? Be self-aware and be willing to silence the *internal voice of bigotry* within. This is so important because understanding removes pre-judgment; compassion motivates us to action; and validation will help to heal the wounded heart. You see, neurologically speaking, what we believe and what we do for the good of others feeds back into our own brains and *heals* us. When we think right, we do right and, therefore, experience an internal peace.

As you read the following true-life experiences and the viewpoints of different cultures, you will see that prejudice is a worldwide epidemic. It is a belief system that shames others in order to exalt self. You will see that prejudice is not exclusive, but infiltrates and separates anyone who is or believes differently. Each one of the following individuals desired to share his or her story with a heart for healing and reconciliation. You will hear from men *and* women from various generations, with diverse ethnicities and cultures, and all with different religious beliefs and socio-economic lifestyles.

Real Life Stories Reveal the Pain of Prejudice

Harold

"My family experienced racial prejudice. Our family lived in a predominately white community, and I attended schools that were over 90 percent white, which brought many challenges. Because of the color of my skin, I remember not being invited to birthday parties. If a child got upset with me on the playground or in gym class, they would call me a 'nigger.' I even experienced mistreatment from my teachers because of the color of my skin, causing me to act out …I was always in trouble.

"My family also experienced prejudice by our relatives because we lived in an area that was considered 'for whites.' The community was for 'upper class citizens,' so we were called 'bougie'; they believed that we felt we were better than others. My mother and grandparents always dressed me in the best name brand clothing, so when I was with my cousins, they would tease me by making critical comments. It was one thing to be mocked by schoolmates, but another thing to be teased by your own family for being 'privileged.' I was also viewed as talking and acting 'white'. I still don't know how whites act and talk."[27]

Nikevia

"My husband and I are in an interracial marriage; I am African-American, and he is Mexican and Puerto Rican. We have experienced racial prejudice because of this. There was a great deal of rejection from my mother-in-law's family. Many did not accept me and were cold and unwelcoming. A family member said to my husband, 'How do you go from this to that?', meaning how do you date Hispanic women your whole life and then end up with a black woman? They went beyond race to religious prejudice because I was also a Christian.

"My side of the family was open and accepting, but they and 'close friends' made comments saying that they knew I would marry someone outside of my race because I've always 'acted white.'

"In public, we constantly catch stares from both black and Hispanic people.

"My grandfather grew up during segregation and went to an all-black school. He still has the mentality that white people are out to get black people; they can't be trusted, and they think they are better than us. This has always frustrated me because my family as a whole has always raised us to love all people, regardless of differences, and to give everyone a fair chance until they prove otherwise. No matter how much I try to explain to my grandfather that his thoughts are false, he still chooses to stay stuck in that prejudicial mindset."[28]

Donna

"I experienced prejudice as a single parent. I had three children by three different men. My mother and grandmother both had children by different men. Often, I would hear, 'Aren't you Betty's daughter?' I could see their facial expressions, and at times, when walking away, I would see them whispering. People would say that I was fast and easy, that I thought I was cute, and was criticized because of my lighter skin.

"My mother experienced a lot of prejudice growing up. She was bullied because she was light-skinned and small. Her father was Cheyenne and Irish, and her mother was Blackfoot Indian. She always grew up in low-income housing and was shunned because of that. The girls were extremely jealous because of her beauty and falsely accused her of wanting their boyfriends. Hearing those stories made me angry and sad because I was experiencing the same thing as early as first grade.

"Because of my experiences, I believed that all men were alike; they were all cheaters, liars, and users of women for sex, money, etc. What also fed into the belief was my hurt from men growing up through molestation by my stepfather and his three brothers. I felt that you cannot trust any man!"[29]

Kevin

"My brother and I, plus one other student, were the only three people in the elementary school of the 300 to 400 students who were of Asian descent. We had to ride the bus to and from school. The bus ride was about 20 minutes. There was one older kid on the bus who would make fun of me because I looked different. He would ask me why my face and nose were so flat. Kids would pull the sides of their eyes and speak fake Asian language to point out how I looked different from them, until they got to know me.

"My parents, brother, and I would walk along the sidewalk, and people we didn't know would shout across the street, trying to imitate speaking in Chinese and shouting out racial slurs. Back then, items made in Japan were of cheap, low quality. My parents would teach us to just ignore them.

"When I went off to middle school (junior high school in those days), we were segregated by academic levels and would change classrooms to move to where our teachers were, and my peer group accepted me. I earned respect from performance, so I learned to cover shame with outstanding performance and work-based results.

"In Boy Scouts, I excelled at most activities and quickly became a leader. But there were some who never associated with me or my dad, who was a volunteer leader. I remember dating a girl in middle school for a short time, but I never met her father because he apparently hated Japanese people (I think because of World War II). Her dad was a Boy Scout leader in our troop.

"Today, I do not necessarily face outward prejudice. Although I am considered a minority, so when I serve on corporate committees, they get to check the box that the committee was inclusive."[30]

Kevin's Reverse Prejudice

"My first experience working a government contract involved developing the personnel database for the U.S. Marine Corps. Because of the data involved, we compiled statistical analyses about gender, race, ethnicity, and other demographics. Because there are over 150,000 active-duty Marines, the sample sizes are large and statistically significant. I remember seeing that the Asian group scored statistically higher on the intellectual exams and taking pride in that. A type of reverse prejudice, as if to prove to all of the people that made fun of me growing up that I had a right to be respected. This was a kind of self-defense mechanism. It would take many years to process through the unhealthy thoughts of work-based self-worth."

Kevin's Father

"When my father was in second grade, his teacher refused to let any Japanese students go to the bathroom, so many of them wet their pants. This was before internment.

"Of course, in response to the invasion of Pearl Harbor on December 7, 1941, over 100,000 people of Japanese ancestry were relocated away from their West Coast homes inland to concentration camps. My parents and their families — both the Ikeda and the Hada families — were relocated to the Posten camp in Arizona. There are a ton of stories.

"Because no one knew what was happening, neither the government nor the families, the Japanese families didn't know if they should sell their property or not. Some did, some didn't.

"Our great-grandmother sold her lettuce farm in Salinas, California to seven men who each became millionaires (Bud Lettuce Farm today). She died poor. All families cooperated with the government (i.e., there were no protests) and were shipped via train to concentration camps located in the desert with barbed wire and guard towers with armed guards. They moved into the barracks and used rope and blankets to make 'rooms' to separate families, making the best of the situation.

"Japanese American young men volunteered to serve in the U.S. Army and formed the 442nd Regimental Combat Team to prove their loyalty to the United States. The 442nd became the most decorated unit of size and duration in the history of the U.S. Army.

"When the war ended, Charles Seabrook worked a deal with the U.S. government to relocate 4,500 Japanese Americans from concentration camps to work his commercial farms in southern New Jersey. He built low-cost housing and schools for them.

The Japanese Americans Citizens League was formed to represent the voice of Japanese Americans in the U.S. government. My dad served as chairman of the Philadelphia Chapter, organizing events to solidify and socialize the Japanese American families."[31]

Monique

"Presently, my family lives in a West African nation. There are so many cultural beliefs and traditions that affect our family daily, for good and for bad. For instance, many men will not submit to women in leadership positions. Many women are mistreated in their homes and by society. I have heard men refer to women as if they are trouble makers and a burden to the men that choose to marry them. In parts of my nation, they call young girls who are extraordinarily gifted and intelligent witches rather than valuing and celebrating them.

"There is also prejudice concerning skin color, believing fair is more beautiful. The fairer-skinned people are better, cleaner, and smarter. Some employers even hire fairer-skinned people above darker-skinned individuals. Our older sons have experienced prejudice from their own people simply because they are natives and not internationals. We have gone to public places and the workers insulted our sons in their local dialect. They have been asked to leave the table because they are darker-skinned and couldn't belong to our family. Though our sons said they were in our family, they were accused of lying and told they were not suitable to be in our family."[32]

Anna

"In my country of origin, my mother has experienced prejudice in her job. The country she currently works in has a lot of east Indians, and she is looked down upon at times because she is black. In their thinking, black means you are not qualified to do the job."[33]

Johanna

"I grew up on an island that has various races, and I never thought much about race. Though I knew there was prejudice, I had bigger issues to deal with. It was not until I came to the United States that I recognized how black I was. For whatever reason there is strong race-consciousness and many assumptions about other races that are not entirely true. I was aware of my ethnic background before I came to the United States, but it was magnified once I came here. Upon my arrival, someone said to me, 'I didn't know if you were going to hunt for your food or if you would buy it.' I chuckled to be polite, but I informed them that 'we didn't swing from vines in the Caribbean.' I worked past that experience, but remember thinking, 'Do you think I'm a monkey or something; how could you say that to anybody?' When an individual has these types of experiences, they carry it inside themselves subconsciously, causing their mind to automatically believe that others believe the same about black people. Without positive interaction, it could cause you to become prejudice yourself.

"Also, growing up I was abandoned by my father and abused by another father figure. That caused me to believe all men were bad and selfish. Though I had a desire to be married, I was terrified of marriage because of my beliefs concerning men. Even when I did marry, there were places of fear that I had to overcome. I remember saying, 'Men are ********.'"34

Annette

"My grandparents told stories about themselves and their family after slavery had been abolished. They and their family would work on the land as sharecroppers for an entire year. At the year's end, they would go to collect their pay and were told that they still owed money. I remember feeling that they were cheated of a year's earnings for which they had honestly worked so hard. Though slavery had ended, I felt that we were still in slavery, just another form.

"In the 1960s, when I was in the fifth grade, we were told that the smarter African-Americans would be sent to Northeast Middle School. So, we were bused miles from our middle school so that we could integrate. The Caucasian children did not want us at their school. They spit on us. They fought with us. We would fight back, but only the black children would get put off the bus. If we sat beside them, they would push us off of the seats. They called us monkeys and told us to go back to Africa. We could not drink from the same water fountains. We had to go to the balcony to see a movie or go to the drive-in. We could not try on clothes in the department stores. We could not eat from the lunch counters. We had to go to the back of restaurants and order food while whites sat inside. We were constantly called negative names. Even when the black dolls came out, I asked why the same doll that was white had a lower price than the black dolls. They let me know if I wanted it, I would just have to pay the price.

"In 1971, my brother was secretly dating a white girl. When this was discovered, he was expelled from school, and we woke up in the morning to find a burnt KKK cross on our lawn and our yard filled with cards saying, 'KKK is out to get you!'

"After I was married, we went to Danville, Virginia to go to Value City. When we got to the Virginia State Line, our son had to use the restroom. We stopped at a service station that had a restroom, and they told us that blacks could not use it. So, we pulled off the road to let our son go in the woods, and the white men at the service station shot a gun for us to move out of the area.

"In the 1970s and 1980s, we would go with the church on picnics. We would go to a popular lake or to the beach. They would not let us or our children change in the locker rooms. We had to put up towels on the bus windows to let the women and girls change at one time and do the same for the men. Also, in every store that we entered, we were followed around like criminals because they expected us to steal."

Annette's Post Office Experience

"I passed the Post Office exam and was hired. I started a Bible study there, and they told me that the federal government and religion could not be mixed. They told me that I could not sing or even hum gospel music while working the line.

"The Post Office was hiring a lot of blacks with bachelors, masters, and doctorate degrees. Our supervisor would stand at the clock each night and tell us that he had a third-grade education, and he was over us. He would then say that the KKK (Ku Klux Klan) could bomb that area and get rid of a lot of blacks.

Yes, the Post Office hired both white women and black women at the same time, but the black women were in the trucks dumping and loading sacks of mail that often weighed more than us. They would send the white women upstairs to key in mail. It was said to me, 'You work like a horse and I requested that you and your cousin [also female] work loading trucks.'

I went to the Labor Union, but nothing changed; I faced even more harassment. I then went to the Postmaster General in Washington, D.C. and he flew down and inquired why this could not be resolved. At that point a supervisor came to me. (All of their stress had me experiencing mild heart attacks.) This white supervisor said that he was going to get me out of the Post Office if he had to make me have a heart attack and die. And he said, 'You can tell whoever you want, but it your word against mine' as he pointed to his 'white' hand indicating…"[35]

Annette is only one year older than I am. All these blatant, arrogant, and bigoted actions and attitudes towards her and those she loved are, to quote my grandson, "**stupid**!" This injustice, though in her past, still wrecks my heart! This past **abuse of power** for the silent generation and the baby boomers is still screaming in the ears of today's young people. Their hearts carry a hurt, a secondhand indignation, for what their ancestors experienced.

Annette humbles me. She shared how her experiences caused her whole life to be consumed with prejudice, and she, in turn, grew to dislike white people. Later in her life, she knew she was called to pastor and saw herself as one who loved everyone. She began to realize that she had to remove racial prejudice in regard to whites. She chose to ask forgiveness for her prejudice and chose to forgive those who treated her with such disdain. Her heart's desire today is for everyone to see that we are brothers and sisters, for all prejudice and profiling to stop, and for us to choose to love unconditionally.

Eva

"My parents and grandparents told me how they were denied jobs because of their race. Many of them lived through the Civil Rights era, when schools were first being integrated, and they were told by whites, 'We don't want you niggers in our school.' They were called 'monkeys' and other derogatory names, being treated less than human. They bore the pain of ignorant statements like, 'The negro is intellectually inferior.' Some of them actually believed it, until the Civil Rights Movement and the rise of Black Empowerment Groups worked to restore the dignity and pride in 'being black.'

"My grandparents told me stories of traveling from Florida to New York to pick fruit. They said they would pack food for their trip because many restaurants and stores would NOT serve them food because they were black. They told stories of how they couldn't drink from the same water fountains as whites. If a white man addressed you, you couldn't look them in the face or assert yourself. My great-grandmother told me a story about how her dad's brother was sold to another plantation in Georgia, and he never saw his family again. There was such loss, grief, and fear that affected our family generationally.

"I experienced a handful of whites in my elementary school, along with white teachers, while living in Florida. I liked them. They were nice to me, so I was nice to them. However, my school in up-state New York, which was predominantly white, caused my sister and I to feel a little odd as two of the four blacks who attended the school. My teachers were nice there, but the white and Mexican kids seemed like they had never seen a black person before. I had very few friends. I remember in an after-school program, an older Mexican boy walked up to me and asked for my hand. He bent my fingers so far back until I cried. Even though I had that bad experience with a Mexican boy, I never developed a prejudice towards Mexicans, and my community never warned of friendships with Mexicans, only whites.

"I remember my family car breaking down in a parking lot in southern Maryland. A car full of white boys saw us and started circling our van yelling, 'niggers … niggers … niggers!' My grandfather got his shotgun ready because that is the way we lived, ready to take on a white person."[36]

Caroline Johnston

"Waking up to the thunderous sounds of bombs was a normal occurrence in Northern Ireland during the 'troubles.' Prior to this, the country was largely united but became extremely divided with a deeply embedded prejudice in the minds and memories of the people. Clinging to past wars, misunderstandings, and cultural ties perpetuated the unease and non-acceptance of the other side. Segregation led to sectarianism, which in turn led to daily shootings and bombings. I clearly remember British soldiers lining the streets and wondering how these barriers of sectarian bigotry could be taken down and how the civilians would survive this war zone.

"The political tension turned into a war of religious denominations as hatred festered over the years. The Catholic and Protestant rivalry was a cover for the core political debate. Republicans thought they were justified fighting for a United Ireland, and the Loyalists defended their connection to the United Kingdom and the royal family. Arrogance, pride, and mistrust led to bigotry, infiltrating the whole country, especially in the inner city, working-class communities. There was also a lack of willingness to communicate with the other side leading to a repetition of death and destruction. A wall was constructed in Belfast to keep apart rival factions, but this only served to perpetuate the hatred of the other 'side.' Murals were painted over the walls to give each side a sense of identity. On the Republican side they proclaimed, 'Our day will come' and on the Loyalist side, 'If you don't love it, leave it' and 'No Surrender.'

"After over 30 years and countless bloody atrocities had been orchestrated by all paramilitaries, some brave leaders stood up and called for a peace agreement and disarmament. At the same time, hope was beaming through fully integrated and inclusive schools, such as Belfast Royal Academy, where I attended. Our principal stated to parents, 'If you are uncomfortable with your child sitting beside a person from another religion, then this school isn't for you.' The inclusive approach that adopted no tolerance for prejudice developed a new era of acceptance and peace. Cultural exchanges gave Northern Ireland children the opportunity to stay with an American family and another child from the side they were never exposed to. It was an enriching program that changed the mind set of many and contributed to a new understanding. As John Maxwell affirmed, 'Diversity is a good thing, we are all partially right and all partially wrong. The only way to transform the world is through diversity, not just by one party.'

"In the past, it was risky to be in certain areas of Northern Ireland with the 'wrong' accent. An Irish Times article illustrated some interesting facts, following a documentary on cross border visits. Northerners who visited the Republic for the first time realized they were surprisingly similar, with the same sense of humour and the same spirit of generosity. Stepping across the now-unpatrolled, invisible border allowed them to discover, communicate, and connect with the other side.

"Forgiveness has been the key to restoration; it has helped reduce the fighting, tearing walls of hatred down, and, in turn, building stronger communities. The greatest leap toward faith was in the 1990s when Sectarian leaders and former leaders of terrorist groups agreed to a ceasefire, entered into talks, and became political leaders representing reconciliation. During a business meeting, I agreed to shake hands with one of these reformed terrorists, which was a challenge, knowing that he had orchestrated numerous murders and had blood on his hands. I chose to put the past behind me, as many others were doing to unite our country.

"A more poignant example of forgiveness is my close friend, whose father, a police officer, was murdered by a terrorist group. Although it hurt, her forgiveness set her free from what could have been a prison of bitterness that so many remained trapped in. The scars of the past remain for some, but it is evident that the peace process has brought prosperity to Northern Ireland. Its streets, once filled with rubble and ashes, are now splendid and covered in beauty. Loving our neighbor as we love ourselves is the key to sustained peace.

"We have a long way to go, but I believe the great people of Northern Ireland and the Republic of Ireland will win this war of prejudice.[37]"

Norm Interview

Norm and Nancy graciously invited a mutual friend and I into their beautifully quaint home. They appeared to love life and each other as their five valued babies — two small pooches and three large Greyhounds — surrounded them, all of whom greeted us with much enthusiasm and many kisses. When the dogs calmed, we all positioned ourselves to hear this valued man's story.

Norm is a Russian Jew. While he does not consider himself religious, he directed my attention to the beautiful menorahs displayed on the mantel of his fireplace. He reached behind his shirt to reveal his necklace — a Star of David, a six-pointed star symbolic of Judaism and Israel. In his hand he held a paper penned with memories, which was evidence of his thoughtful preparation. His personality was strong-minded and unwavering, yet he was vulnerable and transparent as he spoke of the pain of anti-Semitism that "only a Jew can understand."

Nancy is Norm's third wife, and the day following our interview, they would celebrate their 25th wedding anniversary. His first wife was Jewish. Before he married his second wife, he felt his first sting of prejudice as his German soon-to-be-father-in-law said, "I don't really care if you are a Jew. Just take care of my daughter." The passive sarcastic tone of his comment made clear his disapproving, prejudiced thoughts on Norm's heritage.

The father of Norm's two stepchildren was a bigoted influence. As his wife was making matzo ball soup one day, Norm's 7-year-old stepson insolently said, "I'm not going to eat this Jew food."

They later moved to a rural community where they were beautifully welcomed. Friendships quickly developed as dinner invitations increased. They returned the kindness and welcomed their neighbors into their home. This particular neighbor lived right next door to them. When he saw the Jewish star from the Torah on Norm's desk, he simply said, "I didn't know you were Jewish." That was the last time the neighbor talked to them.

Later, as Norm was struggling and going through a difficult divorce, a friend encouraged him to go to a Christian minister who was wonderful and loving. He went to him many times, as well as to a convention requested by the minister. Upon his return, the minister said, "Are you ready to convert?" Norm said, "No, I am not converting." The minister's response was, "Then I can't talk to you anymore." This was hurtful and disgusting to Norm because he recognized that, "He didn't care about me as a human being. He only wanted a conversion."

Authentic honor is the heart to value another amid our differences.

When Norm and Nancy began to grow close, her brother said, "You need to find a Christian, not a Jew. Stick to your own kind." She wouldn't speak to her brother then and continues to reject him 27 years later. After Norm and Nancy were married, his mother-in-law was in their home when they were not there. She was trying to find a needed household item during a snowstorm and called Nancy's sister to ask about it. Her response was, "What do you expect from that cheap Jew bastard?"

You might think, "What's the big deal?" Maybe you were expecting the horrors of the Holocaust to be a part of his story, and this seems insignificant. We cannot marginalize the effect of hatred, prejudice, bias, and bigotry. These life experiences hold the power to impact a person's entire life.

At the time of this writing, Norm is 76 years old. He communicated, "I'm just cautious ... careful." He has learned to keep his ethnicity a secret in order to protect himself and Nancy from anti-Semitic hostility, discrimination, and prejudice. He began to share current events of anti-Semitism. He said, "All you have to do is go back to 1938 and go over to Germany to find out what it was really like. Almost all the Germans became anti-Semitic, and all the Poles became anti-Semitic. They killed my people." He said, "I'm not going to walk outside with the Jewish Star and say 'here I am' ... I am living in a neighborhood where I am the only Jew.[38]"

What These Stories Reveal

Our automatic patterns of thought are the result of long-term memory that is developed through repeated experiences. We also know that the communication of information from others, especially when it affects us emotionally or triggers fear, trains our brains to think and believe a prescribed way. Therefore, when we hear stories from those we love, when combined with our own personal experiences that support that information, our brain becomes imprinted with a long-term memory that can be taken from the subconscious to the conscious at a moment's notice, causing us to relive the emotions again and again. When we experience a traumatic event, memory is instantaneously etched in our brain as the pain of that event immediately activates fear-based memory.

Pre-judgment locks me into a former reality as we rehearse the fear, the powerlessness, and the pain. These dreaded emotions cause us to run from anything that is remotely similar to our past experiences. Who puts their hands back in the fire after being burned? Science explains that when we,

> Replay painful incidents mentally, or dwell on hurtful events, and negative feelings begin to crowd out possibilities and you may drown in a sense of [injustice]... The brain's basal ganglia stores every reaction to severe disappointments. And if negative or bitter — those reactions limit your chances for finding well-being in a similar situation.[39]

I was the youngest child with four older brothers. I was not the girly-girl with the princess dresses and would have never been caught playing with dolls. I climbed trees and did what the boys did. When I was small, my brothers wanted me to ride a horse, so I signed up for this new adventure. When my brothers put the saddle on the horse, they accidentally forgot to tighten the straps sufficiently. When they placed me on the calm horse, it began to walk. As the horse's gait increased, I began to bounce on the saddle. This was all fine until the saddle turned completely upside down on the horse. I was immersed in total fear holding on with every ounce of strength I could muster. All I could see was the horse's legs, and all I could hear was my brothers' yelling. They ran after us and stopped the horse; there was no harm done ... or was there? It was not a big deal for my brothers, but to this day, I still do not ride horses. A horse stable borders our land; I love sitting on my front porch looking at the horses frolicking with each other or simply grazing, but I have absolutely no desire to ride them. Over 50 years later, I see a horse and remember that experience.

I remember as a 3- or 4-year-old, my daddy went into the attic of our little home nestled in the hills of Pennsylvania. He came downstairs telling us about the large black snake that was living in the house. He found the snake wrapped in the rafters, and it bit him. It was not a big deal to my dad because black snakes are not poisonous and are good because they eat mice. I, on the other hand, was horrified. I would rather see a mouse than a snake. The attic was right above my bedroom!

Hidden in the woods there was an old stone mill that was reduced to rubble and infested with snakes. As a young girl, I was violated at that mill. That specific memory is very vague because I was so young, but I clearly remember the trauma of seeing a den of snakes.

It is safe to conclude that my thoughts, attitudes, and beliefs about all snakes is now simply, "The only good snake is a dead one!" Even into my adult years, if I saw a picture of a snake it instantly stirred a sense of fear. My brain was imprinted with instructions for my protection!

There were also mindsets that were developed inside this little girl's mind from these and other experiences. Mindsets were formed from my experiential reality exaggerating the truth. Subconsciously, these events began to tell me, "If I can't trust my brothers to protect me on a horse and if I can't trust my dad to remove a snake from our home, then I must protect myself." The well-kept secrets of sexual violation were held in their own storehouse of tainted reality. The truth was that my father and brothers loved me and desired to protect me. However, my fear and my *perceived* lack of protection were writing pre-judgmental beliefs within my mind. Powerlessness and fear was the buried core of my thoughts and emotions; therefore, I adapted my behaviors to only trust in my own power. My personality was assertive, focused, and determined even as a little girl because that is what I needed in order to meet my needs. We call this survival.

Eva spoke earlier about the Mexican boy who took her hand and bent her fingers back so hard she cried. She wrote, "I was only 4-years-old at that time. I and my sister were too young to fight him." But, then she adds this statement, "The next school year, I became the bully and beat every child I could. I was always in trouble, and I was only in kindergarten."[40] Out of fear and a sense of powerlessness, she became the bully rather than the bullied. This was her survival.

This fear produces a *fight or flight* response, which is important if we are facing physical danger. However, our brains do not differentiate between a physical threat and an emotional threat. For years I lived ready to fight all men — especially white men. Eva had to fight whites, Mexicans, or anyone who threatened her survival.

I am not advocating aggression or making excuses for the prejudice in our world. However, it is important to understand the reason why the majority of the world's populace are affected by the epidemic of mistrust and the symptoms of fear and ignorance associated with prejudice.

> *Love is innate at birth, but prejudice is learned.*

Prejudice is simply fear-based pre-judgment. When we believe, act, and respond without knowing someone personally, or react to a situation without gathering the facts, it is prejudiced by its very nature. That is why I believe there is prejudice in all of us. That is why I am convinced that if we, as leaders, assess ourselves objectively and confront all pre-judgment, bias, and the loudest voices in society, our decisions will be healthy and purpose-driven. We will find ourselves making better decisions, enjoying healthy, diverse relationships, and taking risks that will empower success in our personal and professional lives. What valuable partnership could I sidestep because of pre-judgment? What effectual door of opportunity would I close out of fear? Is my sphere of influence restricted and incomplete because I only connect to those who are like me and endorse all my ideologies?

We have to possess the courage to silence the internal voice of bigotry in order to live life fully and impact our world for good!

With the understanding that prejudice is a learned mindset, our brain can be rewired to its innate nature — love and validation — by changing the way we think.

For our own emotional health and the health of our spheres of influence, we must embrace the courage to be a part of the solution and refuse to feed into negative, fear-driven narratives.

Today's Choice is our Place of Power!

We often gather together within our little cliques of camaraderie, stay safe in our circles of familiarity, and construct our little band of brothers. We understand, relate, and have similar experiences, which brings a sense of validation, belonging, and acceptance. The need for community provides a family where we can give and receive love and protection. This is beautiful and every person on the planet should have the ability to enjoy this place of mutual support and encouragement.

These relationships are so valuable because from this place of empowerment, we should emerge to enjoy the benefits of diversity, inclusion, and life-long discovery. We were meant to live life fully, pursue noble endeavors, and expand our relational horizons to know more, and become more, than we ever dreamed possible.

Is it feasible to have genuine healthy and positive relationships without sharing similar experiences or understanding? Is it possible to enjoy reciprocal relationships of value, honor, and celebration when we come from a different reality? Is it a prerequisite to fully comprehend another's battles, struggles, and pain in order to care deeply and commit fully? Can we team together as instruments of justice on behalf of our society when we have come from different worlds?

Yes, because the choices of today are our place of power!

Powerful people change what they can and choose peace in what they cannot.

There are things we are powerless to change. We cannot change our past experiences and respond differently through our present understanding. We cannot go back in time and muster the courage to go through the doors that our shame and fear kept us from. We cannot go back and negate our stupid actions as we lived for-the-moment or succumbed to peer pressure. We are also powerless to control the attitudes or actions of another — past, present or future.

There are things other people are powerless to change! They cannot go back in time or negate the stupid mistakes of their past. They also are powerless to control those within their own race, family of origin, generation, sex, or platform of influence. Why would we judge an individual for something that they are powerless to change?

Attacking people for their past failure is a place of prejudice. I personally do not want to be judged for the immature decisions of my youth or the reactive and attacking self-protective outbursts of my insecurities. I do not want to be judged by the injustices of my race. I do not want to be judged by the actions of leaders who abuse their power. They are not me; they are the opposite of whom I am!

Today is our moment of power! Today's response to unchangeable things demonstrates how secure and powerful we are on the inside. It is counter-productive to justify what we cannot change. However, we can take responsibility for our present choices and position ourselves for a better, more impactful future. It is at that point that our external world begins to change for good.

CHAPTER EIGHT
Rumors, Gossip, and Slander

The majority of people worldwide are living under a shroud of mistrust concerning the influencers in their society. People cannot trust media networks or the printed word to speak without bias. Their opinion is masked as news, their sources anonymous, and their objective is to influence the masses. Rather than simply entertaining, there are very few movies or television shows that are not inundated with an agenda to proselytize for a subjective ideological agenda. Opinion without truth is already prejudiced.

It is necessary to research what you read on social media to see if it is fact or fiction. The ability to trust leaders has become increasingly difficult because self-driven motives are exposed daily as their intentional twisting of truth comes to the light. All these are acts of injustice and an abuse of power, but they are tolerated because of subservience to money and a power-driven agenda. There was a day when gossip was ignored because it was just Betty Bucket-mouth or Bigoted Bob. Today, this has become so commonplace — and extremely influential — that rumors, gossip, and slander have gone viral.

One of my favorite classic movies is *White Christmas*. Watching it was an established tradition in our family when my children were young. The movie's plot focuses on Phil helping Bob find a wife so he can get a break from their rigorous performance schedule. A little romance was beginning between Bob and Betty when the gossiping housekeeper, Emma, decided to listen into a phone conversation. Bob genuinely desired to help the former army officer, General Waverly, and was arranging the details to honor him. Emma only heard portions of the conversation and believed that Bob was taking advantage of the General. Emma, who couldn't help herself and was a busybody, reports her partial and false conclusions to Betty, causing Betty to believe a lie. Betty was so angry and left suddenly, leaving Bob in a state of confusion. It all worked out when Betty learned the truth. The movie ends beautifully as Bob and Betty kiss and all sing the holiday favorite, "I'm Dreaming of a White Christmas[41]."

Partial truths can be as destructive as an outright lie. Rumors, gossip, and slander hunt for a seed of truth and pervert it. It is pre-judgment — prejudice! We hold to faulty beliefs because we focus on isolated experiences, or partial truth. *All* rich people have it easy. *All* poor people are lazy. *All* Muslims have an evil agenda. *All* Christians are judgmental. *All* young people are entitled. *All* black people hate whites. *All* white people are privileged. *All* men are perverts. *All* women are manipulators. This could go on and on.

> *When we stereotype a group of people, we choose to believe a lie*
> *about the majority.*

I have learned the truth that all men are not perpetrators. In fact, I have been married over 40 years to an amazing and honorable man. He has been the biggest cheerleader in my life. I am surrounded by men of all ages, races, and vocations who are honest, integral, and trustworthy! If it weren't for partnerships with these men, my success would be sabotaged.

I have learned that all women are not gossips, petty, or manipulators. The truth is that I am surrounded by talented and intelligent women who have hearts to impact their world for good!

I have learned that not all governmental leaders are abusers of their platform, but most genuinely and sacrificially pay a huge personal price for the good of others. I have spent time with statesmen — male and female — who are humble, teachable, and trustworthy.

I have learned that not all popular personalities, celebrities, or sports figures use their influence to divide. Many work tirelessly to use their platform to be a voice of hope, healing, and unity.

> *Each person is an individual! It is unfair to judge someone through your past experiences with others or through the experience of a third person.*

I am sure that you have experienced betrayal and/or rejection by someone you entrusted with your business or your heart. I understand that pain and the resulting fear to trust again. I've learned that I can protect my heart by focusing on a higher purpose. Years ago, I adopted a truth that has served as a safeguard to keep me from putting walls of suspicion around my heart. If I am not close enough to be hurt, I am not close enough to make a difference.

Will we allow a few bad apples to taint our view of all? Will we allow another's experience or opinion to pollute potential partnerships? Will we allow gossip to poison our belief about another?

I have learned that rumors, gossip, and slander can distort my reality. I have made a decision to not allow them supremacy in my thought-life. Everyone should be given the right to be viewed as innocent until proven guilty. Many times I've heard others slandered only to learn it was false or distorted. Knowing the truth gave me the opportunity to enjoy valuable friendships. I have also learned the painful facts and discover some to be dishonest and disingenuous; therefore, I choose to deny them access to my life and heart. I draw healthy boundaries concerning that individual.

> *Having a no-gossip policy grants us the access to love life.*

Anti-gossip Activist

I have hated gossip from the time I was a young girl. It is amazing how you look at your life and recognize a golden thread of purpose woven within the tapestry of your heart and soul even from childhood. My core internal motivator is justice; its expression was evident in ways that were uniquely conveyed even from my youth.

When I was 9 years old, we moved into town, where we had neighbors living in close proximity. An old lady who lived next door was gossip personified. She never had anything nice to say about anyone. She was quick to expose and spread rumors throughout the neighborhood about anyone and everyone. I still cannot imagine what was happening on the inside of her that caused her to enjoy exposing the hurt, pain, and battles of another. I cannot connect to her addiction to crisis and chaos and can't imagine how she could possibly be entertained by the devaluation of others.

As a teenager, it made me so angry that I had to do something about it; I just didn't know what to do or how. I was taught that we were to respect our elders and never show disrespect. However, wrong is wrong at any age! Gossip is wrong at any age!

Back then, sauna belts had just become popular. This heavy plastic belt wrapped around your mid-section. It had a tube with a mouthpiece to blow it up with air. You would go out into the heat and the objective was to sweat off belly fat and gain a slimmer waistline. Well, I now had the perfect strategy and tool to confront Betty Bucket-mouth's gossiping.

It was a hot summer day, and our grass needed mowing. I had a two-fold purpose that day — to mow the lawn and to give this meddlesome neighbor something to gossip about. I put the sauna belt around my waist and blew it up as much as it would allow. I covered myself with a large smock top and began slowly mowing the lawn while looking very pregnant. I waited to make sure she could see me as she glared from her window. I mowed along the fence between our houses, giving her the needed ammunition to gossip and spread rumors in order to slander my reputation.

Operation Gossip-buster was a success! Within days it had spread throughout the neighborhood that Melodye was pregnant. Of course, her words were quickly debunked; she was exposed, embarrassed, and undoubtedly displeased with this disrespectful teenager.

Let's think about this. What if I had been pregnant? What if this were true? What benefit comes from shaming a young teenager? What benefit would come from harming my reputation?

This woman's slanderous nature was etched in my memory. Years later, when my actions were shameful and could be substantiated by a gossiper, I met another old woman. This woman was different. She refused to judge or condemn me, even when it would have been easy for her to do so. She is also etched in my memory but for a different reason. She was willing to believe in me when I didn't believe in myself. At 21 years old, I decided that one day I wanted to be a little old lady like her. Love and kindness will make the better role model every time.

My Definitions

I have created my own definitions for the following words based upon the pre-judgmental damage of each action and their expressions.

Rumors: Unconfirmed, unproven, and speculative statements spoken as if they were factual in order to influence a desired outcome.

Gossip: Manipulative idle talk to sway the opinion of others against someone or something, most often benefiting the one who gossips.

Slander: Purposeful character assassination in order to stimulate mistrust and sabotage another's success.

Each of these deceptive and manipulative actions is conceived from the seeds of pre-judgment, assumption, bias, and stereotypes. Whether the expressions are diabolically motivated or are a manifestation of passive-aggressive behavior, the results are injurious. Each of these is a devaluation of a person and an exaltation of self and egocentric motivations. Each is destructive on every level and are, once again, an abuse of power — injustice!

Printing a passive retraction, offering a meaningless "sorry," or passing the buck saying, "That is what I was told," does not magically remove the damage done.

Gossip, rumors, and slander are injurious to a person's reputation, but also to their hearts.

A beautiful young woman, whom I will call Emily, knows the pain associated with assumptions that lead to gossip, rumors, and slander. She writes,

> When I was 18 years old, I was falsely accused of abusing a cousin. It all started with a false rumor from a friend's mother claiming I said that my father abused me. I confronted and told them my father never abused me.[42]

This would have been the perfect time for her friend's mother to apologize and make it right with those with whom she had shared this damaging gossip. Instead,

> She then went and talked to my aunt who replied, 'I think she abused my son.'

> The accuser alleged that I abused her son when I was 13 years old, but it wasn't until I was 18 that the accusations began. The drama, emotional stress, and fear continued for six years. I never knew when another letter would arrive with new accusations or when the police would come to my home and question me again. When the police would come, they would always leave saying, 'I don't understand why we were called here in the first place and nothing that the accusers are saying appears to be true.' Because of these calls, I had to go to the police station for fingerprinting.

> The entire community turned against me, so I rarely left my house so I would not be seen in public. I went without sleep, but when I did, I was plagued with nightmares of the police taking me away. I worked with children, and while the case was pending, I was unable to be seen in public holding or touching a child. After six years, thousands of dollars, and many days in court, during which my accusers never made a court appearance, they finally acknowledged that there was no truth in their accusations. It was thrown

out of court, but it has left me with the painful process of physical and emotional recovery. After four years and choosing to forgive my aunt and her family, I must continue to work at rebuilding the trusted reputation that I once enjoyed. Now, I am starting to believe that I could be a mom to my own children one day. I am so thankful that my husband walked with me through this painful journey.[43]

How can we challenge the important things when we indulge in mindsets that devalue and dishonor one another? How can we care for our fellow man in authenticity and purity if we do not silence the internal voice of bigotry? Is it justice — power used for good — to be judgmental of others? Or to believe the worst about someone when we hypocritically foster internal discrimination and are predisposed to inequity?

If we choose to align our thoughts with truth and justice, our emotions, attitudes, and actions will follow suit. If our hearts are pure, we won't have to worry that our hidden thoughts will slip out of our mouths. When we have integrity of heart and soul, people will know that we are trustworthy and that we value them.

How do You Respond to a Gossiper?

I am sure by this point I have made my disdain for prejudice and devaluation known. I want to be a leader who uses my influence to motivate others to silence the internal voice of bigotry. I also want to have the courage to be an advocate for those subjugated to all forms of injustice.

I have traveled and heard the derogatory remarks from one nation's people made about a bordering nation. I've heard one leader criticize another because of differing methodologies. I've witnessed people relish the failure of another while acting personally superior. At one time or another, we all find ourselves in these situations where what is being said around us is far from uplifting. What do we do when we are thrust into a gossip-filled dialogue?

Positive affirmation: When negative words are spoken to us about someone, one of the most powerful and influential things we can do is to respond with an assertion of validation. This is our first line of defense to protect our own thought-life. This actually silences the internal voice of bigotry because we do not allow the unconstructive words to take root in our minds. Neuroscience teaches that when we reject a thought it will not establish neural-memory in our brain.

Additionally, the moment we choose to validate the person or group who are being spoken against, our words establish a healthy boundary, informing the gossiper that they are not permitted to speak that way in our presence. This is a gentle correction that clarifies our stance and also challenges them to correct their thinking.

> *We can't control the negative attitudes or actions of someone, but we can cut off our agreement.*

Most people will stop at that point, recognizing that you are not welcome soil for their seeds of idle communication. Others, however, may try to justify what they have said, prove their point, or protect their ego. What do we do then?

Verbalize the boundary: If someone persists in trying to degrade or devalue another, clearly present your boundary lines with kindness and respect. Sharing with the person, "I am not comfortable having this conversation" communicates to them that you are not interested in entertaining their gossip.

> *There will always be those who try to control your actions to meet their needs, require your endorsement to their opinions, or pressure your judgments to validate theirs. Choose wisely — your actions determine your path!*

I'm a big proponent of boundaries. My husband and I transformed our two-car garage into a spacious playroom for our grandkids so that they have a space where they can enjoy themselves. With that, however, we also created boundaries for the rest of our home. They are not permitted to run and jump throughout our house however they please. They know which rooms they can rough-house in and where they must channel their energies in a "gentler manner." This allows them to have fun while protecting my house! This also communicates that we love and respect them and that we expect them to respect us in return.

Often, I travel to nations where it is common for landowners to have concrete walls surrounding his or her property. Many hire guards to keep them, their families, their property, and their possessions safe from intruders and thieves.

Proper boundaries are not cruel or restrictive; they are a reflection of wisdom and sign of value for what you have.

Boundaries keep the good in and the bad out. Gossip, rumors, and slander are all intruders that violate our emotional health. We must diligently guard our thoughts, emotions, and beliefs so that our attitudes and actions are beneficial and not harmful. It is not unloving or unkind to verbalize a boundary; in fact, it is the most loving thing we can do for both the gossiper and the subject of that gossip.

On very rare occasions, an ardent gossiper will rise and fight. They will get angry; you will quickly become the bad guy. You will promptly move from being a friend and ally to a targeted enemy. What do you do?

Do not defend yourself, simply separate yourself: It's important to defend others, but don't waste your words defending yourself. Human nature wants to protect and defend ourselves when we are under attack. Of course, I agree with self-defense if there is a physical attack. However, in order to maintain my internal peace, I have learned not to defend myself against an ego-attack. The more powerful and poignant action is to separate myself from the gossiper.

Don't waste emotional energies on critics, cynics, or things beyond our control.

I have no power to control another, nor do I desire to. However, I do have the ability to separate myself from a negative conversation. In the organizations that I lead, we have a "no gossip" policy. Gossip is unacceptable, and, because we foster the safety of our community, people quickly learn that gossip is not welcome.

This does not exempt us from difficulties and challenges. However, when there is genuine honor for one another, we can work through anything. If someone is inclined to be addicted to crisis, it is likely that they will quickly become uncomfortable in our culture.

When useless drama knocks at your door, don't answer! Protect your emotional energies, your internal peace, and your God-given purpose. The treasure within you is too valuable to waste on man-made crisis.

The Emotional Damage of Gossip

The most loving thing I can do is confront gossip, rumors, and slander. In doing so, it is with the heart-motive of restoration. According to neuroscience, we can reject the reception of negative words spoken by others. This prevents thoughts (electromagnetic light impulses) or memories from being established within us. However, for the one speaking those fear-based negative words, his or her thoughts activate the words which feed back and reinforce the negative established memory in his or her own brain. It has a boomerang effect. While I can choose to shield myself from being a target, the one lobbing insults is inadvertently placing the bullseye on his or her own head.

While speaking on bullying in a public school, I used neuroscience to illustrate to the students what destructive bullying does to the aggressor. As I shared how every word feeds back into one's own brain, building fear-based memory, one young man spoke out loudly, "Ohhhh! I'm not going to do that anymore!" The class laughed at his response, but he was absolutely serious! I later heard reports that incidents of bullying decreased within the school. When people recognize that their actions are hurting themselves, they will be more inclined to deal with these internal saboteurs.

This holds true not only for gossip, but also for thoughts, attitudes, and actions of prejudice, assumption, bias, and hatred. Everyone is a loser in the prejudice game.

What if I am the Object of Gossip?

Being the object of gossip or prejudice is familiar territory for many. This is sad, but true. Gossip and criticism always make us feel violated as we want to fight and defend ourselves from the onslaught of character assassination. The closer the relationship — personally or professionally — the greater hurt we experience. What do we do?

Reject the fear-based negative thoughts: A core need for healthy neuro-functioning is to be loved and validated. Gossip is a direct affront to our worth. We must make a conscious choice at the moment of an ego attack to reject the negative thoughts and attitudes in the words spoken. This means choosing not to rehearse, think, or repeat these harmful words. You are powerfully not allowing them to take up residence (build memory) within your mind-brain. This is not easy, but it is worth it to protect our emotional health. We hold the power to protect our minds from these words of character assassination.

Find your calm and consider what was spoken: Through the years, I have learned to deny my instinctual propensity to get angry with the person who now feels like the enemy and look deeper than the hurt I experienced. Even though I know what they said was harmful and not true, I still have to choose to assess myself in that moment. Did I plant a seed through my words, deeds, or attitude that sent a message I did not want to send? The fact is, we only know what we know, and we do not know what we do not know. Is it possible that I am missing something? Is there something

I do not see? What was my body language portraying? Were my emotions heightened? Could it be that I did not handle the situation with wisdom?

There have been times when I went to a trusted friend who I knew would be completely honest with me. I asked them for feedback to determine if or how I may have sent the wrong message. This is where courage and humility are needed in order to take personal responsibility to repair the relational breach. I must know that the person is more valuable than my pride. I've learned through the years that it engenders respect when I acknowledge where I was wrong.

One day, I was talking with my right-hand woman. I was frustrated and overwhelmed at all the work that was on my plate. I was irritated and communicated some frustrations and complaints. As soon as our conversation ended, I felt horrible because I dumped negative garbage right into her lap. I recognized that my attitude was fear-based and powerless. This was not my finest leadership hour. I immediately called her, asked her forgiveness, and let her know that what I said was totally unacceptable. She graciously said, "I know your heart." She was mature enough to not allow it to penetrate her heart; however, I am responsible as a leader to practice what I preach and create an empowering culture. As my team and I actively model a way of mature communication, it allows for mutual respect for one another and represents a healthy influence to those we lead.

Leading by example will build trust and substantiate the personal commitment to the mission we defend.

Let it go: It is good when people arise to defend you, but protecting your ego is often counterproductive. If you have objectively examined your heart, words, and actions and have found yourself without reproach, do your best to let it go!

This is not to say that we should tolerate others devaluing or abusing us. This is unacceptable in any personal or professional relationship. However, when it comes to protecting ourselves from what others think or say about us, we do not want to waste our emotional energies on what we are powerless to change.

Picture a 32-ounce bottle that is filled with all the emotional energy you can spend in a 24-hour time period. Where do I want to spend that emotional energy? Do I spend it on petty gossip or leave room for the possibilities of the day? Will I focus on fear-driven emotion or on focus-driven purpose? The moment I try to control someone else, I am wasting my emotional energies and will likely spend my precious time ruminating over something I cannot change. I cannot allow distraction, accusation, or external threats to keep me from accomplishing the goals of today or from laying a foundation for tomorrow's noble endeavors.

Disallowing the offense of gossip is an emancipation proclamation for your soul.

I remember how my four older brothers loved to tease me when I was young. They would say and do all types of things to get a reaction out of me. That is what childish immaturity looks like. But we are not children anymore. We are not powerless; we are powerful! We can use our power to walk in self-governance. By not being controlled by the opinions of man or negative circumstances, we will feel powerful because we are powerful. When we walk in self-control, there is no desire to convince or control someone else's thoughts, feelings, or decisions.

If we allow the toxic behavior of another to control our lives, we have chosen to empower their influence and sanction their behavior.

CHAPTER NINE
The Clarion Call

You are officially invited to join the ranks of courageous leaders who have answered the clarion call — the call heard around the world boldly appealing for positive action.

Throughout history, we see iconic men and women standing for justice. What we do not always see, however, are the countless unsung heroes who take on the personal responsibility to respond to injustices when they hear a cry for help.

We may not be able to change the whole world, but we might just be able to change our world — our family, our field, our community, even our nation. Every person longs for the freedom to succeed. We can be a voice to support, encourage, and model the way for others to follow. We can grow to reject every form of pre-judgment within our conversations and our deliberate actions.

Just as there are many forms of prejudice and abuses of power, there are also a **multitude of solutions** to dismantle its impact. We are powerless to regulate another, but we are powerful in what we choose to think, believe, and exemplify in our own lives. Our proper use of this power can and will bring about emotional health, social healing, and cultural strength.

Zeal Without Knowledge

A clarion call requires positive action. Genuine love, validation, and celebration for all must be our weapon of choice! This is what will bring about healing, restoration, reformation, and unity. Despite popular opinion, the end does NOT justify the means. In order for true justice to win, our heart motivations must be for the good of all, including those with whom we may disagree.

As a young woman, my heart for justice led me to a great job at the Federal Bureau of Investigation (FBI) in Washington, DC. Working for the Justice Department was a dream come true, and to be given a position in the laboratory division was beyond every expectation I held for myself. Though I started as the low man on the totem pole, I quickly worked myself to a position where I felt I could make a real difference in the capital city of the nation that I loved.

I held big, zealous dreams, but I was ignorant of so much. Though my skills were perfect for my job, and I had the ability to climb the proverbial ladder, I did not have the conscious awareness of the real problems of our society or the understanding to develop the strategies needed to make a positive contribution. My heart was in the right place, but I did not have the knowledge or the wisdom to make a real difference.

I was a little country girl going to the city with no understanding of urban life, let alone the dog-eat-dog world I was now living in. I had no frame of reference for racial prejudice or putting position and power above the objective of justice.

There was a list of experiences that I allowed to pervert the motives of my heart and hinder my ability to make a difference. The knowledge I gained was painful, so my actions became a release valve for anger and frustration rather than a pursuit of a worthy cause.

I served two agents in the laboratory division. Their cases came across my desk before and after the agents provided their examinations. My daily responsibilities were to process the evidence and prepare the reports for the field offices or law enforcement agencies. All day long, I reviewed evidence and read reports of horrific crimes happening all around me. The job was fuel to the fire of my painful past experiences. Inwardly, I was overwhelmed at the magnitude of the corruption that took place and the acts of violence and cruelty I had to process day after day. Outwardly I held it all together, but soon my heart became a breeding ground of fear-driven thoughts, beliefs, and actions.

I purposed to find a positive release in many ways. First, I went to an all-black section of the city to be with families and their children. A few nights a week, I would go to what was like a community center and make crafts with the kids. I so enjoyed this and the beautiful relationships that were developing. I had no knowledge of the danger I had put myself in until one dream-smashing night. On this particular night, the door swung open and two black men entered the room with such anger toward me. One of them raged, saying, "What is the ******* doing here?"

The coordinator of the inner-city work began to defend me saying, "She is cool!" With that these two men grabbed me by my arms, lifted me off the ground, and carried me down the street, throwing me into a cab saying, "***** get out of here and never come back!" I never went back. This is where I learned that all black men were not like my Kansas City superhero bodyguard. I learned my lesson of where I could or could not go in the city and where I was or was not welcomed. I was heartbroken because many welcomed me there, but the small prejudiced minority ruled with fear and biased intimidation. I grieved much that night because I could not understand why they could not see my desire to contribute. Would the children feel I had rejected them? Who would take my place? My world began to unravel as a daunting sense of powerlessness threatened my dream of making a difference in the world.

At this time I lived on Capitol Hill, renting a very small room,

> ... my finances were limited, so I would walk to and from work. Every day, as I proudly promenaded down Pennsylvania Avenue,

I would pass a derelict that staked his claim right outside a liquor store. He was horribly hunched over and could not straighten himself to stand erect. My heart just ached for him and compassion rose inside my heart as I passed him daily on my walk to work. We never spoke to one another, but we would acknowledge each other through a little nod of the head and a kind smile. I didn't have much money, but when I was able, I would buy him a cup of coffee and his eyes would light up …

I honestly looked forward to seeing him every morning and every evening. I know he also anticipated the humble acknowledgments daily affirming his value. I didn't understand at that time that our brains are wired for love and validation, but as I look back, I can clearly see how my little gestures were a spark of life to a hurting man's soul.

One day, walking home during rush hour, the sidewalks packed with hundreds of people, I saw from a distance my friend lying on the sidewalk. My attention was drawn to this strange image because it was so unlike him. Normally he would crouch down against the liquor store, keeping himself back away from crowds. As I moved closer, I was shocked to see him surrounded in a pool of his own blood. Words cannot describe what my heart felt at that moment! It was a sense of powerlessness, as well as a forceful compulsion to do something, anything!

I have no knowledge of what happened, but my assumption was he had been stabbed or shot. What I did know was that he was lying on that sidewalk dying. I witnessed how men in their fancy suits nonchalantly glanced down and just walked on by, not caring about this valuable life.

I began to yell for someone, anyone, to call the ambulance as one man replied, "He's just a dumb bum!" I ran into the liquor store and demanded they call an ambulance. Once again, the man's words were horribly demeaning! I was furious and terrified at the same time, as I jumped across the counter and said things I would never write in this book, but the store clerk responded, "Alright!" When the ambulance finally arrived, my friend was pronounced dead.

My heart felt like it shattered into a million pieces as I grieved for a friend that I never spoke to and never knew his name. I could not believe that hundreds of people who passed by were not visibly shaken by what they saw, appeared not to care, nor showed any compassion. I cried and cried, unable to find comfort, nor could I reconcile what I had just experienced. I realized that I didn't even have anyone to talk to — no one to trust. Disillusioned, I lie upon my bed that night with a pain so deep, anger so intense, and a profound disappointment in the people and the city that I came to serve.[44]

As I witnessed the hardhearted, callous responses towards a homeless man, I formed my own internal prejudice for a whole city that obviously did not care. If they did not care for that man who lay dead on the street, who was to say they would care if it were me lying there? This is when I made the decision that I had to look out for myself.

One thing I appreciated about working for the FBI at that time was their protection of us. They had stringent rules about our lifestyle, moral conduct, and our strict adherence to procedures and responsibilities. We could never be late for work or they would come looking for us — so no one was ever late! I worked with a young woman who didn't show up for work on a Monday morning. They found that she had been kidnapped on Friday going home from work. She was rescued alive, but the trauma she experienced was emotionally crippling. My passion for justice, my heart for the city and nation, and my ability to love and trust started to become a distant dream as I began to adopt an internal culture of anger, bitterness, and prejudice. At that time, I didn't have mature mentors to help me process my pain in a healthy way. My justice and service-oriented values began to twist into self-protective ideals focused on physical and emotional survival.

These and other experiences drove me to live a self-focused, fear-driven, proud and prejudiced life of assumption and bias. These mindsets became my automatic patterns of thought. I began karate training at the FBI, which was very demanding. I was loyal to my job, and my goal was to advance in my position and make the most of every opportunity to become successful within the organization.

My heart had changed. The zeal that once propelled me to make a difference was dried up. The only justice I sought was my own. I had a rude awakening to the harshness of the world. Alcohol was my anesthesia, and climbing the corporate ladder was my amnesia, covering my innate contribution to the world. I was bitter, angry, and selfish, but I could perform outwardly in such excellence that I appeared successful.

All of this took place because I did not have a firm foundation for my passion and my motivation for justice. I thought that if I could change the world around me for good that it would somehow change me internally. Subconsciously, I believed that if I could bring healing to someone else, it would simultaneously bring healing to me. In retrospect, I recognize my zeal was not established in mature knowledge and understanding. I didn't know what to do with the disappointment, the failure of a flawed society, or the world of imperfect people — of which I was and still am. I didn't have the emotional capacity to know what to do with my past and present pain, shame, or fear. This resulted in frustration and anger; I thought I was fighting for the cause of justice, but my fists were raised in an unjust way.

CHAPTER TEN
The Counterproductive Prejudice of the Political Divide

Politics and parties aside, I write today from my heart, my experience, and my passion for *true* justice. I am a proud citizen of a country that prides itself on being a land of freedom and a home for the brave. With this in mind, I recognize that the legal rights of our nation's citizenry are so often touted, even shouted — sometimes at the expense of those doing the shouting. The fact is that just because one has a *right* does not necessarily mean that these rights are appropriate or beneficial for the participant *or* for the cause they claim to defend.

I've watched the **angry** protests throughout our nation's beautiful cities, the critical attacks from talk-show hosts, celebrities, politicians, business leaders, news networks, and more. I have witnessed different ideologies divide people making enemies of once lifelong friendships. It saddens and concerns me to see that the culturally accepted attitude has become one of combat and resistance, rather than collaboration and partnership. Whether I agree or disagree with someone's beliefs and their legal rights to voice them, the real question should be: are my chosen attitudes and actions genuinely expedient?

I see so many today who, like me all those years ago, are fighting for a cause out of heartaches conceived from the pains of their past. I also see how the courts of public opinion are shaping the beliefs and actions of a grieving population. I see the outward demonstration of an internal battle through every sign and symbol, every vulgar word, act of hatred or intolerance, and prejudice displayed to anyone who does not carry their exact message of "equality."

Perhaps the law of the land supports these rights of protest and so-called freedom, but is my method and negative emotion beneficial? Is it actually helpful to the cause or to the internal emotional health of its participants?

The laws of the land must be enforced when someone crosses the line from communicating his or her voice into the destruction of property or committing acts of violence. No one has the moral or legal right to physically assault anyone.

Once again, I believe each person has the freedom to make choices for his or her own life, but when personal freedom takes away another's, it is inherently wrong and an act of injustice.

Dr. Martin Luther King, Jr.'s dream was for racial equality; he dreamed that all men would be able to sit down together in brotherhood. Most Americans say that they celebrate this champion of justice, but are they also willing to follow his example in today's political climate? Dr. King held fast to the heart of the cause saying,

Violence as a way of achieving racial justice is both impractical and immoral. I am not unmindful of the fact that violence often brings about momentary results. Nations have frequently won their independence in battle. But in spite of temporary victories, violence never brings permanent peace.[1]

Dr. King also said, "Darkness cannot drive out darkness only light can do that. Hate cannot drive out hate; only love can do that."[45]

The political divide in Rwanda's recent history left over 800,000 dead.

In a short two months, from December 27, 2007 to January 28, 2008, a political uprising in Kenya left almost 1,500 dead and hundreds of thousands displaced. I had friends who were terribly affected as villages were burned to the ground and close friends turned into feared enemies.

Congo's political wars left millions dead.

Don't think I am being extreme in my concern for the political divide and the ideologies that give license to violence. Freedom of speech does not include destruction of life. The First Amendment to the United States Constitution clearly establishes the necessary limits to protect all the people,

> Congress shall make no law respecting an establishment of religion, prohibiting the free exercise thereof; or abridging the freedom of speech, or of the press; or the right of the people peaceably to assemble, and to petition the Government for a redress of grievances.[46]

We are free to hold and practice our religious beliefs as long as they do not violate another human being or their rights. We have the right to assemble as long as it is peaceable. Screaming hate, destruction of property, acts of violence, and hindering others from exercising their freedom are not only blurring the lines, but also blatantly crossing them.

At my age, I've seen the balance of one political party to the other. I don't think I have ever wholeheartedly agreed with the entire agenda of any political party. However, to demean, devalue, and publicly promote their destruction is not only prejudiced, but also inherently evil. There can be healthy confrontation about political ideologies, but no one has the right to attack the person and his or her family. I want to propose that we not point fingers or divide, but unite instead by focusing on what we all have in common — we are all human beings with choices as to how we will conduct ourselves and exercise our own personal influence. The purpose of this book is to help us as mature leaders to deal with ourselves by *silencing the internal voice of bigotry* within us!

Objectively speaking — and founded in hard science — we know that every thought we accept produces emotions, attitudes, mindsets, and, ultimately, actions. Any fear-based thought releases harmful chemicals that are damaging to the mind-brain and the physical body of the one processing the thought. When spoken aloud, these negative effects also take place in the minds of anyone who receives what was said. As a result, this toxic neural-memory increases sensitivity to harmful thoughts and damaging emotions. This is outwardly visible through anger, hatred, fear, a sense of powerlessness or victimization, compulsive behaviors, and even criminality.

Due to the prevalence of fear-based, toxic thoughts over many years, the internal personal realities of so many are being displayed through a guise of protest. These angry outbursts do not happen because of an event or even a higher cause, but through a fear-based perception of reality that gives it voice.

> *"Your brain creates your reality ... in life it is not what happens to you that determines what you do or how you feel; it is how your mind perceives reality that makes it so." — Traci Deuz* [47]

This contemporary cultural craze of hate-fueled protest cannot heal the land or unite a nation. Rather, it is damaging to those who have participated and have supported these efforts. Scientifically speaking, we cannot speak hatred without experiencing prejudice and propagating a false narrative.

> *We are critical of what we do not understand and attack what we are afraid of.*

Neuroscience clearly reveals the movement in every DNA strand in our physical body — positively or negatively — via our thoughts and actions. I am grateful for democracy, but what I am witnessing today worldwide will not heal if we continue struggling as we are. These thoughts and actions will only accelerate the negative and toxic mindsets in an already hurting populace. How can this heal?

The anger from my personal pain kept me toxic. It wasn't until I chose to see myself separate from my experiential reality that I began to recognize that I carried an internal strength to be the best I could be in every situation. I was then compelled to do what was right despite the wrongs in the world. I have learned the greatest way to fight — to do justice — for myself and others is to cross the great divide and build bridges rather than burn them in the fire of anger, or even fear.

If we are going to start a revolution or movement, let it be fruitful in building healthy minds, cultivating strong relationships, and becoming carriers of hope, validating our fellow man. We have the power internally to choose extravagance by giving honor, taking time to understand, and modeling before others a heart that is tuned for their good.

The clarion call — the cry for our response in positive action — is being heralded across the land. A sound is being heard inviting millions to rise with a voice of hope and healing. Listen to it and act on it!

Courage is beckoning those who will reject divisiveness, pre-judgment, assumption, bias, and an attitude of supremacy. Respond to that courage!

There is a commission for all to emerge as leaders who use their power for good and stand as voices of justice.

I fervently encourage you to answer this call!

Our nations are hungry for what is right. We can respond to this hunger by doing the right thing with the right heart.

CHAPTER ELEVEN
Confronting Past and Present Prejudice as an Instrument of Justice

The pain of our past marks us, but it doesn't have to define us. We can exchange pain and victimization and instead become voices of justice. We can move from having sheer emotions of anger over prejudice to deliberately and proactively doing justice in our spheres of influence. When I see any type of abuse of power, I feel deep anger. I must recognize, however, that I have to properly direct the anger toward healing and not retaliation. I do not want my anger to be displayed through incongruous means. I hate injustice, so I do not want to become an instrument of what I hate while I am raising my voice and actions against it.

Oppression will never stop by becoming the oppressor.

We can learn to confront prejudicial attitudes and actions by disagreeing with an opinion that is contrary to what is just and right. If someone speaks against a young generation, my response is turning his or her negative into a positive, "I disagree with you. I know many young people who are motivated, passionate, and hard working." To be honest, anyone who knows me would never speak against another race in front of me. I would not be mean-spirited, but I would bring correction to the stereotypical perspectives by speaking about the relationships I have with many different races worldwide.

It is a manifestation of ignorance when someone judges another on the external characteristics of skin color, age, or gender. I did not choose what time in history I would be born, the color of my skin, or my gender. I am powerless to change any of those aspects of my life.

If I could, I would choose to keep the knowledge, wisdom, and experience I have gained over my life thus far, but have it housed in my 21-year-old body. I would choose to have skin that would not burn in the sun, peel in a couple days, and return to the same white it was before the burn. I love being a woman today. However, when I was young with four older brothers, I wished I had been born a boy. I remember thinking that if I were a boy, I would not have been sexually abused.

There are so many things that we are powerless to change. These things bring beautiful diversity to the world. This should be celebrated!

> *Creativity is actualized in a celebratory culture.*

With all of that said, why waste our emotional energies focusing on color, age, or gender when within the package is a valuable treasure. If I am going to dig into someone, let it be to search for the gold within him or her and to help them discover worth, identity, purpose, and potential. I want to be a cheerleader for others so they can comprehend the manner of man or woman that they were truly meant to be. I want to see them become the best version of themselves. That goes for you, as well. Our world needs every person to take their place and release their contribution to the world.

Will we be leaders of justice who are willing to fight for what is right and true? Will we confront evil with a courage and zeal that can impact individuals, systems, and structures? Moral, ethical, and unprejudiced leadership provides a platform to ignite the passion of another's voice. Ultimately, it frees the very atmosphere; it generates a paradigm shift, which activates creativity and productivity, and brings positive change to our spheres of influence.

> *Prejudice was not interwoven into our culture in one day, and healing will take time and deliberate effort.*

We are positioned throughout all realms of society, each surrounded by people immersed in hidden pain. As leaders — people of any realm of influence — can you imagine the positive effects that we could achieve if we lived to be a solution? Can you picture the impact that this would have on families, employees, clients, cities, communities, schools, governments, and ultimately nations?

Present generations are still trying to heal from the effects of ancestral slavery, wars, loss, and personal abuse. We want to help them heal. Our pain and the pain of our ancestors can be a weapon against the oppressors of today. We can be a voice for those who have been silenced by fear and shame. We can choose to see the pain of those hidden from view. I can't change the past, but I can be a voice in the present. My hope is that you will join me in rising up as present-day abolitionists to say, "Enough is enough" to abuse of power and prejudice against our fellow man. Come alongside me as we courageously confront every type of injustice in healthy and productive ways.

> *A champion of justice, Martin Luther King, Jr. said, "Injustice anywhere is a threat to justice everywhere. We are caught in an inescapable network of mutuality, tied in a single garment of destiny. Whatever affects one directly, affects all directly."* [48]

Focus on Your Sphere of Influence

There have been many times in my life where I felt I was only a cup full of solution in the midst of an ocean of problems. When I look at injustices worldwide, I feel so small and insignificant to make a change. The fact is that I cannot change the whole world, but I can make a positive difference in MY sphere of influence. I can make a difference for one, and each single moment of impact has the power to ripple throughout generations.

When I focus on what I cannot do, I feel powerless to be the positive influence that I desire to be. When I focus on what I cannot change, I feel defeated and inadequate. However, when I choose instead to focus on what I *can* do, celebrating those in my life and in my realms of influence, I can be a seed planted into someone's life for good. That seed can grow; it can multiply, and it can become a mighty forest that reaches higher and farther than my hands could ever go. All it takes is that you and I be willing to do the planting.

> *Powerful people protect their inner health; they refuse to be controlled by the hateful actions of another. This gives them the ability to influence their world by loving life despite what they cannot control.*

The people closest to us are looking for someone to exemplify powerful and healthy responses to the drama and chaos that tries to invade our shared world. How we respond to the unchangeable things in life can demonstrate how secure and powerful we are or are not. If we can't control *it*, we cannot allow *it* to control us either. Instead, by choosing to live in our power as personally responsible and mature influencers, we will not only be healthier and happier ourselves, but also modeling a better way for those around us. This is when our world begins to change for good. Right in our own homes, in our workplaces, in every group that we are a part of, we can make a difference by letting go of our inability to change someone else and making the change within us first, paving the way for others to follow.

Family

> *All abuse, rejection, or shaming is painful, but it is a sword through the heart when it comes from family.*

Everyone has a platform of influence, whether large or small. Everyone has family, friends, peers, and/or community relationships of some kind. What would happen in our world if our families were unified? What if family became a place of safety and validation where each person was treated with unconditional love? What would happen if the love tanks of every child were filled by value-generating emotionally healthy parents and grandparents? What if selfishness, criticism, or pre-judgment was removed from our own families?

Many are angrily screaming hate to the world, but their pain began in their home. I know individuals who were molested by their fathers, brothers or sisters, or aunts or uncles. I know people whose parents were so driven to satisfy their own addiction that the needs of their family were disregarded. I know some who never heard, "I love you," "I'm proud of you," or "I believe in you," let alone, "How can I help you?"

Just as my husband pushed through the experiences of his childhood to become a man of honor, I have watched so many embrace the responsibility for their own private world. They took back their power by rejecting a life of survival under the shroud of blame and offense. They have determined that their future will be different than their past. They have watched those who have abused their power in order to take from others and instead chose a life of contributing. They have conquered their pain and have turned it to compassion.

The home holds the greatest capacity to shape a person for good or harm. There was a young woman who I knew from the time she was 7 years old. She grew up in a nation that was war-torn; many injustices took place in both her parents' and grandparents' generations. Despite the many challenges that the family faced, within the privacy of her home she was raised with much love and acceptance. Her parents would do anything and everything to see their children succeed. Years later, during her high school years, she was seduced by a so-called friend and was later drugged and kidnapped into sex trafficking. Her parents and extended family and friends aggressively searched throughout their small nation and found her after a very short time. Within that time frame, this intelligent, beautiful young woman experienced injustice in some of the most dehumanizing and devaluing ways. After this happened, she came to live with me for a couple months to protect her and allow her to heal.

Through the years I have talked with many who have experienced sexual abuse. The pain will often follow them throughout their lifetime. This young woman, however, responded much differently. She rapidly processed through the pain and became impassioned with purpose in such a short time. I personally did not reveal what happened to me as a child until I was 37 years old; others never share their story. Yet, within a couple years, this beautiful justice-motivated girl is a voice confronting sex trafficking within her nation. She is speaking about it in public settings and even on television in order to bring awareness to other young women.

This story illustrates the power of a healthy family. The first 16 years of her life were established in love, security, and health. This event was horrific, but her foundations were strong and secure, empowering her to move away from this atrocious victimization to be a purpose-driven voice for others.

Would we have the hate speech, incivility, and criminality on a national scale if each home was healthy? I shared how my husband and I carried so much baggage into our marriage. When my children were small, I trained them through shame because I was filled with shame. When I finally took responsibility for the condition of my heart, removed the blame, dealt with my shame, and allowed healing to replace my painful experiences, I became a different parent. The first thing I did was to ask for forgiveness from my children — then 14 and 12 years old. From that point, I began to parent out of health instead of fear. I am so grateful that both my son and my daughter have now grown to be mature and responsible members of society.

To change our world, we must first strengthen our families. Rather than putting added pressure on ourselves and expending so much energy in order to provide more "stuff" for our kids, we have to recognize that they themselves are our greatest treasures and we are theirs. Playing together, working together, serving others together — these are all investments that will fill their love tanks fuller than any object or status ever could. This relational connection creates a place of safety and gives them the courage and confidence to be independent thinkers and voices of influence in their world.

Community, Workplace, and Leadership Roles

In times past, I thought it was humility to avoid platforms of influence. This was because of my distaste for leaders who were egocentric and used their influence for self-gain. However, I have learned that platforms of influence give opportunities to herald hope and bring courage to countless lives. Platforms themselves are unbiased — they are neither good nor bad. However, the voice of the person using that platform can propagate either unity or division. We all have to ask ourselves, "How do I use my platforms of influence?"

How do you conduct yourself with your co-workers or those you lead? Are you empathetic? Do you find common ground? Do you support the marginalized in your organization? Do you reject office gossip and refuse to participate in things that lower the morale? Do you remove yourself from any form of combative competitiveness and refuse to climb the corporate ladder at the expense of others?

It is important for us to give our best within our spheres of influence. This empowers us to be a catalyst for positive change in both individual lives and corporate structures. When we use our power for good, rejecting prejudice and gossip, we will begin to watch a healthy culture grow within our workplace.

Earned Influence — Building Bridges

Anger and hate scream loudly and will never build bridges! Most often, the loudest voice is the least credible. When driven by fear-based thoughts and emotions, the ability to make wise decisions is often hijacked. This hinders the power to engender a sense of safety. Unhealthy people are often attracted to attitudes and actions that are harmful to building wholesome relationships. Angry people attract those who are angry, and this provides a sense of justification to one another's self-sabotaging behaviors. Oftentimes, within the marginal ranks of those who live in cultural offense, license is granted to fight for that which is ultimately destructive to emotional health and injurious to repairing the breach.

It is very difficult to trust our hearts to angry people. Throughout the years I have learned that if people complain to me, they will also tend to complain about me. If people are critical of others, they will be critical of me too. If they pre-judge others, they will probably pre-judge me. I used to think that my love was strong enough to break down those walls, but even love is powerless unless it is received.

In order to help heal our families, communities, and nations, we must first be willing to earn the right to speak into someone's life. If I am not willing to build bridges of connection with others, they will be wary of opening their hearts to my investment. Remember that a pioneer is the first to step out; therefore, we have the honored responsibility to give before we receive. This may mean being the one to extend an olive branch in the midst of an antagonistic environment. We are the ones to take the risk of investment even if there is no return.

There is a young man in my life who I am grateful to mentor and partner with today. He is black, and I am white; he is a millennial, and I am a baby boomer; he is male, and I am female. We are different in so many external ways, but our hearts have bridged the gap. Some years ago, before we knew each other well, he called me with a quivering voice and a lot of insecurity because of his experience with abusive leadership. All he knew was the pressure to perform perfectly and felt he had to submit himself to emotional and sexual usury in order to be someone of value. As an adult, married man and father of three, the fear of his leader's rejection kept him bound in emotional subservience. He was required to ask permission when making simple life decisions in order to remain in good standing with his leaders. As a side note: these abusive leaders were of his same gender and race. This is a case-in-point to show that outward characteristics do not reveal the hidden man/woman or the character of a person's heart.

It took great courage for him to call me that day! I assured him how much I valued him and that he could communicate with honesty and transparency about whatever was on his heart. This began a valued relationship that today has grown into a beautiful partnership with him and his family. It was a step-by-step process to earn the right to speak in and about his life. He would ask my opinion, and I would not provide an answer but instead ask him questions in return, like "What do you feel you should do?" or "What is on your heart?" I didn't want him to believe that he had to hold my beliefs or do what I said in order to be favored or valued. I wanted him to become emotionally mature, confident in his ability to think independently, and secure in who he is and what he could do.

I had to be willing to lay the first girder to build a bridge of relationship. I remember one time he called me and asked permission to build a website. My response was, "If you have to ask me for permission to make a decision for your organization, you better run away from me as fast as you can!" There were many seemingly small responses of mutual love, validation, and respect that began to open his eyes to see what an amazing man he was. He has now written a book on his experience and holds an executive position in a well-known lending institution. His marriage and family are now strong. I am extremely proud of this young man!

See, we have to ask ourselves if we are willing to take the first step. Are we willing to prove that we are different than the loud and angry individuals in our position, race, gender, generation, or political party? Humbling ourselves as leaders is the most powerful thing we can do. Brick-by-brick, bridge-by-bridge, we can begin to dismantle pre-judgment.

Use the power of words to create a positive atmosphere.

> We cannot minimize the power of the mind and our ability to choose what we will think, for by it we activate the whole of who we are.

Words create thoughts. Those thoughts release emotions and attitudes that create beliefs that are ultimately made public through actions. We do what we believe, and what we believe is sourced from what we think. Often, our focus is on outward actions rather than the source — our words and our thought-life. Our words have power. With our words we can either create a positive, uplifting atmosphere where relationships are secure or breed a divisive, fear-based environment that gives license to anger. Through the words we speak and the attitudes we display, we will either be carriers of hope or fear, validation or shame, peace or chaos.

With that said, we have to be mindful of our thoughts and our words. They will either be life or death to us and, therefore, to the culture we are creating. Will we continue to waste our emotional energies on prejudice and its many faces? Will we choose to be critical of those who think and believe differently than us? Will we be cynical and propagate suspicion in those who hear us? Will we speak as weak and powerless victims? Will we vent, argue, and express ourselves through the lens of jealousy and rivalry? If we choose this lifestyle, we will construct a communicable disease of oppression wherever we go.

I don't know about you, but I want to get away from negative antagonistic talkers as fast as I can. I do not want them to dump their offensive garbage on my emotional property. I do not want to be drawn into their prison of victimization. On the other hand, if someone desires health and is willing to pay the price to get rid of their garbage, get out of the blame game, and become a solution, I am so willing to support their journey to wholeness. If they, however, want to drag me into agreement with their defeatist mind-sets, I have to separate myself, and quickly.

> *Separating ourselves from toxic people and environments such as pessimism, prejudice, criticism, and gossip will aid in our emotional health and provide spiritual strength to combat external pressures and the inevitable disappointments that life can bring.*

Words and attitudes that are fear-driven release fear-based neurochemicals within the brain and body. This will negatively affect the one speaking, as well as those who hear, think, and believe what is being said. One well-known neurochemical is cortisol. Cortisol surges through our brain and body causing stress, anxiety, and super-sensitivity and is a threat to emotional and physical health. It increases the heart rate and can even cause physical nausea. Cortisol will be released in stressful situations; however, it is also released with imagined danger, confrontation, or fear of the worst possible thing happening. Our brains treat a physical threat the same as an emotional threat — even if it is only hypothetical. Can you see the importance of keeping our minds free of negativity and prejudice?

If my husband or I are contagious with a cold or flu, out of love for each other, we keep our distance. This is not unloving, but actually a demonstration of love for each other, not wanting someone else to develop the same illness we have. We also have a standard in our home that if my husband begins to speak negatively, I will respectfully correct him. The same is true if I am having a bad day and my words are not healthy, in love, he will correct me. We want the culture of our home to be established in peace — one where a life of drama is unacceptable. We know that powerful people choose peace!

The primary way for each individual and our nation to be healed is by using our words to generate a life-giving atmosphere! When kind words are expressed from a caring and empathetic heart, they become light to the dark regions of the soul. Kindness is not just being nice, being politically correct, or agreeing with pre-judgments and gossip to avoid making waves; kindness is saying and doing what is best for a healthy exchange of life and ideas.

In the early years of our marriage, my husband said, "There are a lot of great women out there, but you excel them all." Many years later, I still remember where we were standing when he said that to me, how it made me feel, and the respect I felt towards him. Just recently my husband randomly expressed, "I was thinking the other day what a wonderful woman you are!" My heart just melted with his validating words. Even though we have different points of view on many things, our mutual love, value, and respect for one another have truly united our hearts.

Health-giving words release a creative power to the recipient to think differently, positively. No matter what we have experienced, we can choose to think constructive thoughts that empower and encourage. These thoughts are an act of wisdom because they will literally rewire the brain from the negative to the positive. Neuroscience calls this neuroplasticity. (I write more on this topic in my book "Higher Living Leadership").

The neurochemical serotonin is released when people celebrate our achievements, speak honorably, and act in validating ways. It is also released when we witness a good deed or see someone do the right thing. Serotonin activates so many parts of our human brain as a sense of well-being, and happiness floods our thoughts. It causes us to feel confident and optimistic towards life. We become more focused and have a greater ability to be a creative problem-solver. Serotonin even brings health to our physical heart! The makeup of our DNA and the wiring of our brains compel us towards validation. Our response literally creates health inside and out.

This life is the only one we will ever have, so we do not want to give power to prejudiced mindsets that lower our quality of life and negatively impact our world. We live in a world of great diversity and a multiplicity of experiences and perspectives, along with all the dynamics of what we cannot control. Either we are going to navigate our life's journey embittered or emboldened to be a healing agent of change. Our life story is not yet complete. We do not want to judge the chapters of our life that are not yet written based upon a few bad chapters of our past. We have the ability to leave our world a better place than we found it.

Powerful People Give Mercy

The person who is quickly offended wastes their emotional energies on things they have no power to change. Be a mercy-giver and let it go.

It hurts when we are judged harshly. We think, "If they knew the whole story, if they knew why, they wouldn't be so quick to judge." There have been situations in my life where I have chosen not to communicate the whole story in order to avoid exposing someone for public scrutiny, even at my own expense. I have purposed to process other's actions based upon what I knew of their life story. I make every effort to take the high road of mercy because I remember my past, my stupid years, my unjust actions, and the anger I lived in. I might have deserved judgment, but instead, caring leaders had mercy on me and addressed my unhealthy actions without judging my heart.

> *Separating the person from the problem is a form of mercy. It does not justify the action, but it provides an opportunity for the one willing to make a change.*

The fact is that I am not you; I will never fully understand what you have encountered. The fact is that you are not me; you will never fully understand what I have had to contend with. Have you ever experienced a group of people trying to convince each other that their pain was the worst? Everyone wants to be understood, but the fact is…

You don't know what it is like to be sexually abused — unless you were.

You don't know what it is like to be enslaved — unless you were.

You don't know what it is like to be addicted — unless you were.

You don't know what it is like to be in poverty-stricken — unless you were.

You don't know what it is like to be hopeless, depressed, or suicidal — unless you were.

You don't know what it is like to be bullied — unless you were.

You don't know what it is like to be rejected or betrayed — unless you were.

You don't know what it is like to be fatherless or motherless — unless you were.

You don't know what it is like to be imprisoned — unless you were.

You don't know what it is like to be homeless — unless you were.

You don't know what it is like to be in combat — unless you were.

You don't know what it is like to be targeted because of racism, gender prejudice, or age discrimination — unless you were.

The list is unending!

We all have paid an arduous price to obtain something that we value. We all have suffered disappointments. We all have experienced circumstances beyond our control. We all have endured injustices. It is true that some experiences are more horrific in magnitude than others, but we do not want another to suffer pain so they are able to relate to ours. It isn't a competition.

Will we be prejudiced towards someone simply because they do not know what it is like in our world? Will we be courageous enough to cross the "you don't know what it is like" gap to partner together for a cause greater than ourselves? There is a propensity to be critical of what we do not understand, therefore, we must choose to hear, learn, and empathize. Even if we cannot come to an agreement, we can come to validation! Competition will cease when we care enough to build a bridge and cross the great divides that separate even when we do not know what it is like. We must decide if we want to be right or have relationships.

Some who have written their stories of prejudice in this book are closer to my heart than some of my extended biological family. We partner together and learn from each other's experiences; our realities are expanded because we do life together. When we move across the racial divide, we realize that there is only one race — the human race! When we courageously cross the generational and gender divide, we see our insights, mindsets, and skillsets that complement each other for a united purpose. There isn't anything we cannot overcome when we choose mercy over judgment.

CHAPTER TWELVE
Your Voice — Your Responsibility

My desire in writing this book has been to confront the destructive power of devaluation of human life in all its forms. My dream is to see a cultural shift in families, communities, and nations so that future generations do not live in fear. I have purposed to write with a heart of value and honor for every person on the planet, even when they have expressed their past and present pain in destructive ways. I've shared with you only some of my pain and mistakes. I am far from perfect, and though I'm more whole than I've ever been, I'm still a work in progress too.

With angry voices, biased assumptions, media propaganda, gossip, and more, there is so much vying for our attention and affecting us each and every day. Every person's reality has been shaped by their own painful experiences, but still there remains a hidden cry for inner peace, emotional health, and personal happiness.

Championing justice will not heal the heart, but the healed heart will champion justice. Confronting what is wrong in our world will not fix what is wrong in us, but internal freedom will confront injustice through just actions. Antagonistic word assaults will never make one internally powerful, but the powerful provoke healthy dialogue and give birth to reformation.

Nelson Mandela was a champion of justice and a peaceful nonviolent anti-apartheid activist. He reshaped history by becoming the first black president of South Africa and later won the Noble Peace Prize. History reveals the injustices against him and his people through a racist governmental system. I have no doubt that there were times he felt like his voice was ineffective, his labors appeared pointless, and his heart was broken. This courageous man said, "A brave man is not he who does not feel afraid, but he who conquers that fear."[49]

Taking responsibility for the possible, or what I can do, is the tiny seed planted in the land of impossibility, or what I cannot do. The more of us who accept the commission for the healing of our land, the greater harvest we will possess for generations to come. Many are fighting to save the planet from destruction and we should steward all our resources well; but, if all our natural resources are preserved and the people themselves are prejudiced and hateful, the affliction of the soul will destroy the quality of life for those on the planet.

In Kevin's account (Chapter Seven: The Painful Stories of Prejudice), he wrote about his parents and grandparents who were housed in the Japanese internment camps. When asked about solutions he said,

> I think the example of the Japanese-Americans during World War II is an example. They took a very long-term approach to slowly work within the system to earn respect and bring justice. Finally, during the Reagan Administration, after almost four decades, the U.S. Government officially apologized to the Japanese-Americans for interning them in concentration camps.

You cannot dismiss the painful prejudice they experienced, but the Japanese-Americans took personal responsibility for their voice, their lives, and their posterity.

> *When our hearts are bound to the pain of the past our capacity to enjoy the present and prepare for the future is limited.*

A strong spirit is not created by painful experiences but by taking personal responsibility for them and using those experiences to shape our internal voice. My life was negatively affected by the pain of my past, and my heart breaks today for the pain of others, but I cannot be bound to that pain. I alone am responsible to silence the internal voice of bigotry within me. Once again, my desire is to see healing come to the people of the world, but the things that I am writing are powerless to change anyone until they take responsibility for the condition of their own soul.

The obstacles of yesterday have no influence in our lives unless we listen to their voice. Let each of us take responsibility to silence pre-judgment, bias, assumptions, gossip, stereotypes, and criticism so the powerful contribution of our voice to impact our world for good is not polluted.

Own Your Life

You must first assume full responsibility to become what you want to see in your world!

In a world where many are affected by the abuse of power, injustice, and even culturally acceptable devaluation, we can accept the fact that we will never entirely escape its diabolical influence. However, though we are not exempt from the force of this influence, we must courageously and powerfully own our life.

We hold the power of choice and internal self-governance. We can choose love when hate is screaming in our ears. We can choose peace when chaos surrounds us. We can choose to reserve judgment and gather the facts rather than gossip. We can choose to judge a person based upon their character rather than the color of their skin, their gender, their age, and even their past. All of these things are unequivocally powerful!

Reacting out of fear, ignorance, and inflated emotion is powerless.

Negative emotions are an ever-changing stream traveling the circumstantial landscapes of life; don't trust them when charting your course.

In order to own our lives, we must reject the blame game, even when it is another's fault. Face it, rarely would human nature accept responsibility without a developed internal ability to own his or her own life. We do not have power over the actions of another, but we do have power to choose how we will respond.

When fighting matches arise, even in the family unit, it is founded in blame. "You made me angry when you did _____." "Why should I show you love when you do not respect me?" The blame game gives away your power to someone as you allow them to regulate how you will think, feel, and act. You will live extrinsically controlled rather than exercising your ability to own your life through self-control.

The choice is ours: we can live out of control, powerless lives excusing our own negative behavior by blaming our actions on the failures, mistakes, or actions of another; or we can own our lives by choosing to take control of self and do the right thing.

We will be taking back our lives by assuming responsibility for our own thoughts, attitudes, and actions. The years of sexual molestation in my life could have held me in an emotional prison my entire life. My shame, fear, and self-protective control would have continued to sabotage my life, my relationships, my leadership, and my ability to enjoy life. I would have allowed the injustices of my past to define my present and my future. I would have continued to parent my children in shame and protect my heart from a good husband waiting for him to inevitably hurt me.

At 37 years old, I realized I was still giving power to the individuals who violated me more than 30 years earlier. Some were dead for many years, yet in my mind their actions against me controlled how I thought, believed, and acted. At one significant eye-opening moment, I realized the anger I was experiencing was not directed toward the people who had committed injustices against me but toward myself because I continued to give those painful experiences power. No more! I began to take back my life.

If you want to stop the influence of the prejudiced, the gossips, and the bigots — own your own life!

If you want to render the actions of another powerless — own your own life!

Assuming Responsibility Through Forgiveness

To own our own life, we must forgive. We believe that our anger, judgment, gossip, or hatred protects us from being hurt again, but the opposite is true. When we remain bound by toxic mindsets that are self-destructive, we begin to implode under the weight of powerlessness. These negative thoughts and stress-filled emotions keep us bound in a prison of self-destructive unforgiveness negatively affecting our physical and emotional health.

Dr. Ellen Weber says,

> Stress comes from hostility — and while it gets dubbed by many names, stress shrinks the brain and anxiety drains mental life. Simply stated, stress flips your brain into shutdown or shotgun mode … You may have defaulted to ruts or triggered further problems … [because] stress from unforgiveness masks as a savior, but strikes as a killer! [50]

Why would I want to hold offense towards another when it ultimately sabotages my ability to be physically, emotionally, relationally, and even spiritually healthy? She continues, "Brainwaves slow to a grind and serotonin supplies diminish under excessive weights of a grudge."[51] We need high levels of serotonin and recognize that a healthy mind brings health to the body; therefore, it's time to "man-up" by asking for forgiveness and genuinely extending it to others.

It is important to understand that forgiveness does not excuse destructive behavior, nor does it mean you have to position yourself in harm's way again. However, forgiveness allows your mind to release another to his or her choices, while you choose those things that are beneficial to your own emotional, physical, and spiritual health. It moves you internally from the sense of being powerless through the actions of another, to a place of inner strength no matter what their attitude. Forgiveness does not mean you are to continue to trust the untrustworthy, but it removes their power to control your thoughts, mind, attitudes, actions, and reactions.

There are such amazing benefits to brain health when we forgive. "When we forgive, we set a prisoner free and discover that the prisoner we set free was us."[52] Forgiveness literally cleans up the memory, allowing healthy memories to flourish. "When you forgive, the very chemical structure of the brain changes from the negative to the positive, affecting the entire thinking/memory building process."[53]

> Forgiveness literally alters the brain's wiring — away from distortions brought about by the past, and beyond fears that limit the future. It leads from misery of a broken promise, to wellness that builds new neuron pathways into physical, emotional, and spiritual well-being.[54]

Forgiveness transforms the haunted ... into healthy...[55]

Reject the Temptation to Be Offended

Someone may send you an invitation to be offended, but you do not have to accept it.

My skin pigmentation is so light it has left me with the constant challenge of protecting my skin from the sun. When I was young, I hated being so white that I would spend countless hours sunbathing trying to get a tan. Often, I ended up with sun poisoning, leaving my body covered with blisters. The sunburn was so painful and my skin so hot that I shook involuntarily with chills. My skin was so sensitive that the slightest touch would cause me to scream, "Don't touch me!" I was so angry that their touch caused me pain that it triggered my instinctive response to throw a punch to hurt them back.

Victim mindsets hold us captive as we develop emotional sensitivity to the slightest infraction as we scream, "You've offended me!" We want to attack the offender and watch them suffer in the same way their words touched the sunburned areas of our life. You might say, "Melodye, you do not understand, they don't know what it's like, they don't know what I've been through, they don't know ..." Yes, this is undoubtedly a true statement — they do not know. However, the only way they will know how you feel is if you tell them.

In those sunburned seasons of my youth, I learned to lift my hand as a stop sign and say, "Don't touch me because I have sunburn." They would respond with compassion and not touch me until I healed. Could it be that our rejection of offense would open a door for dialogue, allowing a perceived threat to become a loyal friend? We are often offended by the actions of another because it is mirroring a wound in our own lives.

"Let your hopes, not your hurts, shape your future." — *Robert H. Schuller*

Separate Yourself from the Rat Race

The rat race is a term used to describe a frustrating and powerless way of life. It encompasses competition, rivalry, comparison, and the idea that this race cannot be won. This leaves us with the belief that something is wrong with us and we are not good enough. Yet, if in some way or somehow, we could be one of the first to cross the finish line, we would be able to stand on the platform and receive the accolades of the masses. Can you imagine the sweetness of that victory? Can you imagine the thrill of seeing the shame and defeat heaped upon all those who have opposed you?

To believe that someone must lose or fail in order for you to win or that someone must be hurt in order for you to heal is a falsehood. This lie leaves us looking over our shoulder for the competitors in the proverbial rat race.

> *The greatest violation of relationship — personally or professionally — is when our hearts grow cold, vision dies, and we no longer care how our actions affect another.*

Self-centric needs consume our thoughts with little regard as to how our behaviors affect others. Emotional immaturity is put on display as aggressive fits of anger work to manipulate others, all so we can get ahead in this rat race.

We expect this from babies and young children, knowing that he or she will mature and grow into a responsible caring adult. In the rat race, however, we see adults throw their fits of rage, hatred, and entitlement, believing that society should cater to his or her needs. He or she feels they are entitled to win the rat race and stand on the platform of champions.

We cannot afford to become our own standard of right and wrong. When we no longer care what is right or wrong and believe that the end justifies the means, we have crossed the line into dangerous territory. We are perpetuating the problem when we could be a part of the solution. These things are red flags waving before our eyes, warning us to exit the rat race.

Every person must personally assess him or herself and then take responsibility through corresponding action; they must own their own life. From that place of proper self-assessment, they can begin to make healthy life decisions and determine how to become the best version of themself.

When we individually begin to understand our contribution to those within our personal and public world, success will be obtainable because of our self-governing power of choice.

It is true that all of us are running a race. This race requires the courage to be faithful to ourselves, loved ones, and the whole of society. This race cannot be won alone. We need each other. We need our diverse skills, races, ages, perspectives, and so on. This race is one we all can win when we compliment not compete, celebrate not tolerate, understand not alienate, and validate not extricate. In simplicity, we win when we love the person and don't fear the difference.

Pandora's Box

In recent years, good and honorable leaders have faced, and are still facing, unprecedented challenges. They find themselves afraid to lead their organizations in the event that their words could be contrived as offensive or that their decisions may appear prejudiced. So many cards could be played that they find themselves walking on eggshells. Some may take advantage of this fear in order to get what they want, working the system. This will never build healthy relationships or positively impact an organization's culture; in fact, it generates an entombed inferno of divisiveness. The one trying to manipulate by using this card for their gain may get what they want, but it will become a complicated set of problems, opening Pandora's box within their soul and within the community of workers that surround them.

Dr. Martin Luther King, Jr. said, "Man is man because he is free to operate within the framework of his destiny. He is free to deliberate, to make decisions, and to choose between alternatives. He is distinguished from animals by his freedom to do evil or to do good and to walk the high road of beauty or tread the low road of ugly degeneracy."[56]

By now you should know my hatred for prejudice, bias, assumption, and gossip. You know I hate the abuse of power from any leader or person with a platform of influence. This influence does not have to stem from positional power. Many people use their relational platforms to propagate their biases. They may appear to be in a casual conversation, but they tactfully use their words and even their emotions to seed their desired outcome.

Fear drives a person to meet his or her needs even at the expense of others. These actions may profit some temporary reward, but ultimately leave the individual in over their head. They have pried into that which is spiraling out of control. Anxiety increases, which places greater pressure on them to cover their tracks with more self-protective and fear-based actions. What is released from the proverbial Pandora's box hurts the one who opened it but moreover hurts society as a whole.

We are at a turning point in history to reject fear, ignorance, and the many masks of prejudice that are birthed from it. Each one of us has a voice — a platform of influence — and we must take responsibility to do our part in healing the land — not to mention humanity and culture — for posterity's sake. Today is the day and now is the time to reverse the scourge of prejudice.

Hypocrisy is to demand behaviors from others but grant ourselves exception. This duplicity is unacceptable and must be silenced in our internal dialogue. Positive change can begin with a committed minority who will take responsibility to be a voice of hope, validation, honor, and celebration within our world.

Love is Powerful

Love is not sentimental emotionalism; it is a powerful choice to do what is best for another. Love is a conscious and selfless action to serve something greater, whether that is the family, the community, or the nation. It isn't physical affection or romance, but a much greater and deeper manifestation of kindness. It is not easily offended or prideful. It is quick to forgive.

Love is a powerful act that releases emotional health to the one giving and to the one receiving. It brings courage to the heart and empowers the recipient to stand strong in difficult times. Love sees clearly the current reality but also dreams of what could be. It is established in truth and knows what is right, just, and good. Love gives!

Powerful love hates prejudice, abuse of power, dishonor, bias, criticalness, stereotypes, corruption, and every other forms of devaluation. These things are an insult to love!

Relationships, families, organizations, communities or nations have never been divided over love, honor, respect, or validation. On the contrary, love has the power to unite, restore, and heal.

CHAPTER THIRTEEN
The Balance: Healthy Boundaries

In this book, I have written out of the core motivations of my beating heart. I am determined to be a voice to confront injustice and devaluation. I have chosen to love authentically and deeply. However, I have also learned that what I carry is a valuable seed and where I invest must be fertile soil.

While we can choose to love everyone, it is also important to note that the best, most life-giving love and connection is created through healthy boundaries. This means that I can love you, someone I may or may not have ever met, as well as my closest friends. Even still I recognize that the best way for me guard the purity of my love is by honoring the capacity and contribution of my heart through boundaries.

Though we reject prejudgment in a negative sense, we should be aware that there are those who have chosen to devalue what we carry or use our generosity for selfish gain, either consciously or subconsciously. We can be mindful as leaders when those individuals are attempting to rob us of quality of life so we can properly guard our hearts and minds.

Healthy, mature boundaries keep the bad out and permit the good to enter. In the same way we lock the doors of our homes, we must assume the responsibility as the gatekeeper of our heart. It is not prejudgment or intolerant to protect your home or heart from a stranger, someone you do not have experience with. To trust without substantiation of someone's moral uprightness is never wise. In the same way, we should never expect someone to trust us without our willingness to build the bridge of relationship and prove that are motives are pure. Love is a choice, but trust must be earned.

> *To grant full access to everyone is not loving, wise, or healthy.*

We should always assess our own hearts and ask, "Am I a trustworthy person? Do people feel safe with me?" Likewise, we can ask the same of others, "Is it safe to open the door of my heart?" There is a freedom to fully and unconditionally value everyone when we know how to properly set boundaries in our lives. The more trust is established, the more secure we are to grant heart access to someone. The age, race, gender, or social status of a person is irrelevant, but the following questions will help us measure if someone honors what we carry and determine if a person is trustworthy.

1. **Do they avoid emotionalism, drama, gossip, and criticism?** If a person gossips to you, they will gossip about you. If they are critical about others, they will be critical about you.

> *Disallowing the offense of gossip is an emancipation proclamation for the soul.*

2. **Do they honestly and authentically value you?** You invest in, sacrifice for, and protect, what you value. You will never have a healthy relationship or feel safe if you are not highly valued. We must always be careful not to prescribe and too strenuously perceive how others demonstrate their high valuation of us or others. This is fraught with potential manipulation and the attempt to control the actions of others.

> *Without the desire and ability to communicate value to others, genuine relationships and doors of opportunity will gradually disappear.*

3. **Do you trust them to protect your heart?** This coincides with the protection that validation brings. If someone protects your heart, they will not speak or act toward you in devaluing ways. You will trust and know you are safe to open your heart when you discern that your heart is protected.

4. **Do they both give and receive from you?** This is an exchange in life — investing and being invested into. In any healthy relationship, there are benefits and also requirements and responsibilities in word, attitude, and actions. Trusted relationships are never a one-way street.

> *In the final analysis, our ability to receive from and invest into others is a true earmark of a successful life.*

5. **Do they have pure motives and unselfish agendas?** It is so easy to trust when you recognize that you are valued because of who you are and not because of what someone will get from you. If there are outward displays of devotion, love, and generosity for the purpose of getting something from someone, there is no devotion, love, or generosity at all. If outward actions appear honoring, but the inward motives are disingenuous then eventually there will be rejection or betrayal, as some may be using you as another stepping-stone in their journey to success.

> *We all have two choices: take advantage of others and get what we want or give and contribute to others. One destroys trust while the other builds it.*

6. **Do they ask for forgiveness and forgive quickly?** This is so important because no one on the planet is perfect. Therefore, we must live a lifestyle of forgiveness and be humble enough to acknowledge when we have hurt another by asking for forgiveness immediately. If I have wronged someone, a simple, "sorry" is meaningless. We must possess the strength of character to acknowledge wrong

doing and to offer restitution. Many are sorry they got caught or sorry they must face negative consequences, but true repentance is when we grieve over hurting someone's wounded heart. This type of repentance and forgiveness builds rather than destroys.

> *The act of looking past imperfections without judgment is both courageous and powerful; it is a response we also want to receive from others.*

7. **Do they love you without your title, position, or what they can get from you?** It's amazing how many people love you when you are owner of the company, the influential leader, or you could build a platform for them. Others may want a relationship because they are living vicariously through association with a successful person. If the position or power you hold would be removed, would they still want to be with you?

> *Commitment to someone only until someone or something better comes along is usury.*

8. **Do they celebrate your success without competition or rivalry?** What individuals in your life genuinely celebrate your successes? Who is excited for your victories? When my husband and I were first married, we bought a beautiful new car with cash. The jealousy of many of our friends was tangible. However, there was one couple who lived next door to us. When they saw our new car, they were genuinely happy for us. They said, "I just love to see people prosper." They made a very big deal about the car, all its features, and their happiness for us. I will never forget the dichotomy of emotions I felt from two types of people. I decided that day what type of person I wanted to be.

> *Everyone needs a cheerleader championing him or her on life's journey.*

9. **Do they share their hearts and listen to yours without judgment?** Do not waste your emotional energies on critics and don't be a cynic. Who would open the door of their home (heart) for someone only for them to find fault with everything they see?

> *When you celebrate the success of others, you are then ready for your own.*

10. **Do they focus on self-control rather than trying to control you?** The moment you try to control another you have abandoned self-control. It is human nature to pull away from those who want to manipulate you, either passively or aggressively. If my focus is self-control then I have no energy to control another, and it's not in my power to do so anyway. Self-control is a difficult but rewarding process, which builds trust equity fast!

> *We have conquered much when we conquer self.*

11. **Do they possess character, integrity, and avoid toxic behaviors?** Opening your heart to those with a deficit of moral strength, honesty, or emotional health is like providing residence to a poisonous serpent. Only those with a death wish would drink poison. Toxicity is revealed through the chaos and drama that follows these individuals. They will manipulate to get their needs met, believing that the world revolves around him or her.

12. **Do they treat you and others with respect and honor?** Observing how someone treats the prominent as well as the marginalized speaks volumes about their ability to be trusted.

When others can answer "yes" to these questions concerning ourselves, it shows that we are on the courageous path to be a trustworthy partner and solution-maker in our spheres of influence. When we can say "yes" to these questions concerning the individuals in our lives, we have found valued treasures.

Our inner circle, those we share real and vulnerable life with, is relatively small. This is our "tribe" where trust abounds and we are secure and safe. However, we are residents of a big world that needs to experience leadership that stops devaluation internally and models it externally.

This assessment has become a litmus test for me. It has proven itself effective in measuring who I can welcome into my inner circle and, most importantly, my heart. The school of hard knocks has not limited me but has become a place of education and wisdom, so I can do, give, and love more and better.

CHAPTER FOURTEEN
What Can We Do?

The things that have our attention will determine our direction. Likewise, the lens through which we see will decide what we become. When our attention and perspectives are aligned with what we are for, rather than what we are against, our life is filled with purpose and our influence is for good.

When we help those who are bound in oppression, we inevitably stop the oppressor's influence. Just as a small candle can light up a dark room, love will destroy the darkness of hatred, prejudice, and gossip. Being an instrument for the good of others automatically confronts the abuse of power.

Prior to a speaking engagement several years ago, I was enjoying time with the leader of the group. As we talked, a woman entered the room to report to the leader that she was unable to accomplish a specific task that she had been given to do. The leader angrily began to degrade her in front of me. He then appeared proud of himself for the strength of his authority. I became increasingly angry as I witnessed his abuse of power. Appalled by his lack of character and his treatment of this woman, I wanted to confront him right then and there. Everything inside of me wanted to attack him! If this was his response in front of a keynote speaker, how did he treat and devalue those he supervised when no one else was watching?

Had this moment taken place in my younger, emotionally driven years I would have undoubtedly said or done things I would have come to regret. I could have even justified my immature and counter-productive actions as a noble endeavor, an "act of justice"! My actual response, however, was to wait until I took the stage. They had invited me to speak that day, and so I chose to use my platform of influence to provide understanding of what healthy leadership looks like and our responsibility to value all those in our spheres of influence — both those we lead and those we follow. I focused on the light rather than the darkness. I never exposed or attacked the leader or brought attention to the specific situation I witnessed earlier that day. Instead, my words painted a picture of health and validating leadership that stirred the hearts of all those present.

I have learned that putting all my emotional energies into the bad would hinder my ability to do good. Publicly shaming a leader would never bring healing. I needed to model a better way, communicate a different message, and demonstrate what healthy relationships look like — both personally and professionally.

> *We learn much about a person by what they love and what they hate.*

We can become a picture of possibility to follow! Living with personal or second-hand offense never heals. Trying to control the actions of another through fear, devaluation, threats, and slander will do the opposite. Inciting people to anger is not only counter-productive to your cause but also harmful to those who join your movement. Inversely, possessing and propagating a heart for healing will influence others to value all, even if they disagree with another's actions. Every act of kindness is a seed planted to heal our land. Every step in the right direction takes us closer to our objective of a healthy and prosperous nation.

Be a Pioneer

Ideally, everyone should exemplify the courage to think and act in ways that are beneficial for all of society. Imagine a world in which influencers refused hatred and, instead, published a message of optimism through their words, attitudes, and actions.

I am convinced that people are inherently good! The majority of our population displays true decency of heart as they reach out to those in need. Wherever I travel I see people who authentically care for one another, even when they live in the midst of difficult circumstances. Our world is looking for pioneers who inspire others to take personal responsibility for the healing of our land.

I have worked in behavioral sciences for over 25 years and have learned that people act in opposition to their true selves when they are afraid. Fear makes us think irrationally and respond in emotionally charged ways that deny us access to wisdom; it has become the commander of society's soul. When fear is present, truth is hijacked by unreliable emotions and pre-judgments, which results in seeing and believing the worst in our fellow man. On the contrary, however, when fear is absent, we will enjoy the satisfying and enriching benefits of emotional health. When the darkness of ignorance is brought to light, we will witness the safety and security that comes when hearts are defended, protected, and loved.

Throughout history there have been pioneers who charted a course for others to follow. How does the direction of a contentious culture begin to change? It will change as pioneers pave a new way and refuse to conform to the present narrative. The very nature of prejudice is divisive; therefore, we must raise our voice of inclusion, acceptance, and honor. We must be willing to pay a personal price by walking the extra mile, taking the time to understand, and then intentionally choosing validation. A pioneer of this kind chooses to shoulder the personal responsibility of refusing prejudice; they powerfully decide, time after time, that they will not participate in any type of devaluation, no matter how big or small.

Pioneers are strategic reformers of culture who are actively integrated into our society. These are the brave leaders who will redefine, for themselves and for future generations, power used for good.

These forerunners will undoubtedly pay a painful price because many will misunderstand them. These courageous ones reject every opportunity to be bought or sold. They may become the object of gossip, criticism, or accusation. Not everyone will understand the why behind what they do. People's opinions or actions toward them may hurt them at the surface, but down deep they recognize that they are working and serving from the future, or what can be. Their greatest price is rarely seen, acknowledged, or valued by others, but still they continue to give.

Those who are prejudiced will be offended by those who love and validate. Those who do injustice will always be offended by those who do justice. Let them be offended. Even if it costs me something, I would rather offend evil than continue to defend what is wrong by pretending it isn't happening.

Pioneers are much like the entrepreneur who pays a higher price financially and assumes the highest level of responsibility. They put their names on the dotted line, knowing that the *buck* stops with them. They do not know what a 40-hour workweek looks like because their every waking hour is consumed with what they have set out to do. They anticipate the reward for their labors, but also recognize that the road may be long and arduous; they know that there are no guarantees.

Pioneers will make the first step toward peace as they extend the proverbial olive branch in times of conflict. The only way to serve society's healing process is to remember that humanity's core need is to be valued. It is the only way to experience emotional health! It's not just what we receive from others but what we are willing to give. When our thoughts, attitudes, and actions align with this validation, we experience emotional health and are able to generate value in the lives of others. Neuroscience as well as axiogenics, the mind-brain science of value generation, confirms the importance of valuing relationships. In my book "Higher Living Leadership", I provide a more detailed explanation of the scientific connection between our thoughts and their impact on the brain and body:

> Our brain is extremely relational and is a highly social organ. 'Most [of the] processes operating in the background when your brain is at rest are involved in thinking about other people and yourself.'[57] Since our brain holds a hierarchy of value, 'above all else, our re-

lationships with other people have the greatest value and are the greatest source of potential value generation.'[58]

Letting go of prejudice and every thought that is divisive may be an enormous challenge when hate seems to be the loudest voice around us. However, if we pioneer this distinctive lifestyle, life will be good for us and we will be modeling a better way. We will enjoy greater levels of personal peace and emotional health while increasing our capacity to be a value-generator in our world.

Doing the good and right thing is always good and always right!

Refuse to Be Divided

I am blessed beyond measure with trusted close friends and mutually supportive partnerships. There are many whom I mentor but also those who mentor me. I have a beautiful family and a valued extended family. I lead organizations but also serve within other's organizations. In each of these areas I enjoy relationships with individuals who are different from me in terms of race, gender, age, religious background, political ideology, etc. Truly, we are better together than we could ever be separately. We learn and grow with each other. We are not trying to make others think, act, or believe just like we do, but support them in their discovery of their unique individuality and purpose.

Now, the leadership consultant in me does wants to clarify something important here so the pendulum does not swing too far in the one direction. While it is good to celebrate our differences, it is also important to recognize that our partnerships must be established upon a unified vision and shared values. Otherwise, even with all the good in our hearts, we will not progress as a team if we are all steering in different directions.

In our world, it is the minority who are unrelenting in their prejudiced mindsets. The angry voices of rioting, hatred, and violence are a small percentage of the populace. The majority of nations are comprised of amazingly good people who desire to live their lives in peace. Most are generous, justice-motivated, and caring. I am reminded of the horrific terrorist attack on the World Trade Center and the Pentagon on September 11, 2001. In the aftershock of tragedy, good people — the majority — rallied to the aid of the stranger beside them. Day after day, tragedy or not, when help is needed, people around the globe gather around one another to help them rebuild and thrive.

A few years ago, I was asked to bring leadership training to the staff of an inner-city school troubled by all types of prejudice. I later brought classroom trainings for the students. The loudest voice that was heard that day was not my voice, but that of the team I brought with me. I took three young women I was mentoring — one African-American, one Hispanic, and one black Jamaican. We genuinely loved one another and operated in an obvious and authentic unity. They would hug me and say, "This is my Mama!" It was evident that I was not their biological mother, nor did I adopt them legally, but my investment in their lives afforded us a valuable relationship. Our partnership was a picture that spoke a thousand words. We never openly addressed racial tension; we just modeled love, unity, and healthy relationship. Great things happened that day.

"Alone we can do so little, together we can do so much." — Helen Keller [59]

Division is a non-issue when we love others and are convinced that people are inherently good. But what if we don't feel love towards someone?

Over 40 years ago, my husband and I brought so much emotional baggage into our marriage that young love didn't feel so lovely! Our first year felt more like a year from hell than a honeymoon! Divorce (division) was not an option for us; we both wanted to make it work. We knew we could not play the blame game but had to take personal responsibility for our own lives.

My husband was not raised in a home in which love or value was communicated. His father was an angry man, often abusing his authority as the "head of the household." His mother was crippled and powerless to stand against the daily chaos. His young life was dominated by fear, and he didn't know how to give what he never received. He had to fight within himself, to push past what had been modeled before him and live a different life than what he had experienced.

After about one-and-a-half to two years, my husband had an amazing revelation that transformed his life and our marriage: Love is not a feeling, it is an action. When you do the action, the feeling comes. He chose from that point to show love no matter how he felt. As he did, feelings followed, and healing came.

Nelson Mandela said that we can learn to love.[60] Dr. Martin Luther King, Jr. said that, "...there is a law of love in this universe, and if you disobey it, you'll suffer the consequences."[61] Maya Angelou said, "Love recognizes no barriers. It jumps hurdles, leaps fences, penetrates walls to arrive at its destination full of hope."[62] Love is a choice first and foremost. If we choose hate, then we can also choose love, and love is a powerful force to be reckoned with.

> *"Learn to love without condition. Talk without bad intention. Give without any reason. And most of all, care for people without expectation."*[63]

Intentionally Make Investments

Every investor expects a return on his or her investment. Anyone who invests into an entrepreneurial endeavor is expecting high percentages of return. Everyone investing in the stock market has expectations that the stocks will increase and create financial wealth. Every parent who invests in his or her children wants the return to be solid, mature adults who succeed in life. Every husband who invests in his wife desires the return of her respect. Every wife who invests into her husband desires his love in return. Investment and returns, sowing and reaping, giving and receiving — these are all principles that apply to every area of life.

If we are willing to invest into the great divides, we will be a part of filling the gap. When we tenderly invest love into the hotbeds of divisiveness, we can expect love's seed to bring cultural change. When we invest into a valuable life, we will see healing and restoration as they receive what we contribute.

In order to close the space between ourselves and any other person(s), we must choose to do the right thing every time an opportunity presents itself. It is hard for someone to argue with you if you refuse to argue back or do not need to prove your point of view. You can watch anger be defused if you are peacefully unmoved by its ego-attacking aggression. A person who is an intrinsically powerful person is not controlled by the intensified emotions of another; therefore, there is no desire to retaliate. Meekness is not provoked by a frustration, manipulation, or lack of respect. In fact, hatred gets confused when your response is validation of others.

Of course, we all have fallen into the self-protective pit of reacting inappropriately. We want to push when pushed, argue when confronted, or convince someone that we are right! In the fallout after such a disappointing event, our only recourse is to be quick to acknowledge what we've done wrong and ask for forgiveness. It's amazing how a sincere apology promotes healing within relationships.

Find Common Ground

All of humanity has the same core needs. We all share the basic physical needs for food, water, shelter, and sleep. We all need to feel safe, to be loved, to see value in ourselves, and to experience a sense of significance through what we do. Whether we live in the Americas, Europe, Asia, Africa, Australia, or Antarctica, we are more alike than different.

Maya Angelou said, "Beneath the skin, beyond the differing features and into the true heart of being, fundamentally, we are more alike, my friend, than we are unalike." [64]

If I want to build bridges instead of walls, I must find common ground. I need to become vulnerable by allowing others into the injustices, failures, and struggles of my life. Facades melt and masks are removed in the presence of genuine authenticity as we share our life stories. Our sameness is found in the midst of our differences as we realize our paralleled experiences. When traveling, people often view me as someone born with a silver spoon in my mouth and have the assumption that I have never known injustice. The moment I open my heart, however, the invisible wall that stands between us shatters with the reality that we are not as different as presumed.

Permission is granted for open communication through common ground,. This allows an exchange of life, validation, acceptance, and understanding. Initially, where there was pre-judgment and mistrust, we can now discover a new friend — something treasured we would have otherwise missed. I have learned that every barrier can be torn down if we reveal our humanity and grant access to one another.

Whether I am speaking in a corporate boardroom, before international governments, within the educational system, or one-on-one, I share my stories of injustice, struggles, and a long list of failures. This does not discredit me, but rather builds a bridge that connects me to the hearts of those listening, regardless of their age or level of influence. Everyone has failures, disappointments, and relational challenges, and all have faced injustice. When we can touch someone's heart, the walls of separation disappear.

As I mentioned before, when I travel, people often put me — the consultant — on an imaginary pedestal and assume my life is perfect. Assumption about another might not be accusatory or derogatory, but it still separates. I quickly dismantle the assumptions because my words have no credibility when I cannot relate to their world, either professionally or personally.

In one instance, while speaking before a large group of international leaders of various races and religions, I observed that no one was looking directly into my eyes. I could feel an atmosphere of shame over the group as they viewed me as superior to them in every way. When I realized what I was facing, I wanted to cry. No human being should ever feel less than another. Though I had done nothing intentionally to cause them to feel that way, my white skin-color, my platform of leadership, and the nation I came from created a faulty assumption.

I responded to the room with an illustration. "Before I begin the training, who would like $20?" No one answered. I came off the platform, smiled, and laughed. "Come on, someone wants $20!" I saw a woman lift her hand ever so slightly. Yay! I called her forward and when she went to take the money, I pulled it back and began to speak to the $20 bill. "You're stupid, you'll never amount to anything, you're not worth the paper you're printed on!" I crumbled it up, threw it on the floor and melodramatically started stomping on it with a barrage of verbal belittling. I picked up the crumbled $20 bill off the floor and asked, "Do you still want it?" Unsure if she should say yes or no, I continued, "No matter what injustice has been done to us, the evil words spoken over us, the times we were thrown to the ground and trampled upon ... nothing takes away our value." You could hear the sound of validation and understanding sweep the large room with a unified "ahhh!" The message was received loud and clear that we are ALL valuable!

Validation is the key that opens and heals a heart!

We had found instant common ground through my validation. Once they knew I genuinely attached importance to them and they knew the motivations of my heart, I discovered a new family. After each session, these influential leaders came to speak with me, shake my hand, hug me, and even kiss my cheeks. When you are comfortable in your own skin you will want others to live in that same freedom!

"I like to see myself as a bridge builder, that is me building bridges between people, between races, between cultures, between politics, trying to find common ground." — T.D. Jakes [65]

Authentic Empathy

Do we genuinely ask others enough questions to help us know what it would be like to walk in their shoes? The resulting empathy validates the feelings of another and dismantles prejudice, along with the effects of injustice and discrimination. Empathy allows us to experience a shift as someone's story moves from an abstract event to an identifiable reality. When we can relate and connect to another's journey, prejudice has already taken a death blow. Shared authentic empathy is a healer of wounds as pain and its accompanying anger begin to dissipate.

My heart was moved as my husband and I enjoyed a meal with a beautiful African-American couple 10 years our senior. We have a valued relationship with them; our communication is open and honest. We heard the stories of the prejudice they experienced and the fear of being one of the few black kids forced to go to a white school as laws of desegregation were being enforced. We felt the burden forced upon them to 'make it work' in the midst of a hostile environment. We could not change their experience, but we could genuinely care! We shared stories from our lives and experiences. Genuine nurturing of one another was a manifestation of love, which is always foundational to restoration.

Empathy is the ability to connect and relate with what another feels and how they perceive a situation. It allows us to touch people with our hearts and to know the hearts of others. We are often critical of what we do not understand, but empathy has the power to dissipate that criticism, as well as cynicism and pre-judgment.

Incredible things happen inside of us where we understand situations, feelings, and consequences. When we employ compassion, identification, and responsiveness, we are positioned to see from another's perspective. We are able to recognize the emotions that are being experienced by someone else. This is a connection that runs deeper than our differences. If we cannot have empathy, we will never be able to make investments or find that common ground needed to bring positive change to relationships or a cultural setting.

> *Without the desire and ability to communicate, value to genuine relationships and doors of opportunity will gradually disappear.*

Stephen R. Covey says, "To go for Win/Win, you not only have to be nice, you have to be courageous. You not only have to be empathetic, you have to be confident. You not only have to considerate and sensitive, you have to be brave."[66]

People don't always think of empathy as a tool of strength, yet it is. Our engagement with it might just be strong enough to build a bridge that can't be torn down.

CONCLUSION

In order to play a part in reshaping the cultural landscapes, all of us must invest our lives in unprecedented ways. I am convinced that influence used for the good of all will indeed restore hope to the grassroots of our nation and other nations for generations to come.

Pure and honest heart communication is absolutely necessary for us to experience true understanding, impartiality, and tolerance. If we are constantly anticipating overreaction, criticism, or an unwillingness to hear our different points of view, it will be very hard for us to foster healthy, loving, and lasting relationships. We must lay aside any hidden agendas to convince rather than understand, to proselytize rather than have relationship, and to attack a person's views rather than celebrate his or her personhood. All these things reveal that we really do not value someone who thinks differently than we do. We can begin to write a narrative that models the possibilities of disagreeing without dishonoring. We can plant seeds of authentic validation.

If you plant a fruit tree, you can be certain that it will produce a harvest of the fruit of its kind when properly cared for. It can take many years for a young apple tree to bear fruit. Likewise, the "seeds" of love, kindness, validation, and celebration may not always produce an immediate harvest. It can easily become discouraging to sow faithfully without tasting the sweetness of the fruit of our labor. However, we can watch it grow slowly, taking root over time. We can guard it, water it, fertilize it, and protect it knowing that we are tending to an orchard bigger than ourselves, one with the potential to feed both nations and generations.

If I truly value humanity, I must plant seeds of validation in everyone whether they agree with me or not, whether I trust them or not, whether they like me or not. I value others because of my character and, perhaps, even in spite of theirs. The seed of validation carries such a powerful influence that it can transform both the giver and the receiver as it brings about beautiful life-giving change.

In my book, "Higher Living Leadership", I describe the science of validation as confirmed by both neuroscience and axiology. I never wish to promote sheer idealism, but instead what is real, possible, and proven. I have hope for our future, and I hope that after reading this book, you will join me in seeing our dreams of reconciliation come true.

A valued friend, Peter D. Demarest, an expert in Axiogenics co-authors a powerful book with Harvey J. Schoof that powerfully impacted my life and leadership, saying "…axiology is the study of how Value, values, and value judgments affect the subjective choices and motivations of the mind — both conscious and sub-conscious."[67] They explain the difference between neuroscience and axiology: "Neuroscience is the science of how the brain works. Axiology is the science of value and, as you know, value drives the processes of the mind-brain."[68] Science objectively supports the impact of validation to bring health to both the giver and receiver.

Refusing to allow prejudice, bias, or gossip inside of you will be the best thing you've ever done for yourself. At the very same time, you will be planting powerful seeds of validation that will impact your world in an unprecedented way.

Join me as we stop the devaluation of others one word at a time, one moment at a time, one person at a time. I believe strongly and passionately that a movement of validation will change us, and, in turn, will change our world for good.

In closing, I have launched a social campaign to help champion this movement of validation. To join me in this effort to bring healing to humanity and to our land, use #StopDevaluation and let us together be a voice of hope, validation, and healing for our world.

"Be the type of person who leaves a mark, not a scar."[69]

#STOPDEVALUATION MOVEMENT

When we devalue another person in any way, it subconsciously gives us permission to treat them as though they don't matter. When something isn't important, we treat it poorly, harshly, unjustly. When we ignore or deny a person's worth, we treat them with the same contempt. Oftentimes, we don't consider a small thought, mindset, habit, or action as damaging; however, these seemingly innocent fractures all too often create a chasm between our fellow humanity. Friends and neighbors become enemies as we take and give permission to exploit one another's weaknesses and differences, and every single time, pain is caused.

Devaluation is a contagious disease in society, and it must be cured. You and I hold the power to be a part of that cure! The #StopDevaluation movement is a call to action to be an initiator of change. We can be the ones who begin to bring healing instead of harm by bravely seeing the value in ourselves and in others.

What does it mean to #StopDevaluation? It starts with intentionally assessing our own thoughts, attitudes, and beliefs concerning ourselves and others. If our thoughts are not generating value, we have to confront them in our own minds and choose to change the way that we think.

The #StopDevaluation movement is for those who will challenge themselves to be the change makers within culture. This means refusing to participate in gossip, rumors, slander, and bigotry. It means choosing love over hate, knowledge over bias, mercy over judgment, and kindness over insult. It means believing and speaking the best of everyone and confronting in healthy ways those who bring harm. These powerful choices will change us, and we can change our world.

Join the movement.

Follow us on social media @StopDevaluation

ABOUT THE AUTHOR

Dr. Melodye Hilton has developed a unique and personal approach to consulting and coaching that creates a positive and sustainable impact. With years of leadership experience, she works with individuals and teams around the globe as a leadership consultant, behavioral analyst, and executive team and personal coach. Her passion is in the development of people, as she believes that each person has a unique, valuable, and necessary contribution to bring to the table. As individuals develop the internal soft skills of leadership, their ability for both personal fulfillment and organizational productivity exponentially increases.

Dr. Melodye's recognition extends throughout all ages, socio-economic, and educational backgrounds through her work in corporate and local business, government, and not-for-profit organizations, as well as public and private educational sectors. She is a Master Certified Trainer for Taylor Protocols, Inc., training people to discover their Core Values Consciousness in pursuit of personal excellence and happiness. In addition, she has served as vice-president of a not-for-profit corporation for over 35 years and founded the International Training Center for the development and equipping of leaders. Dr. Melodye's core passion for justice (power used for good) led her to establish the Voice of Justice Foundation to aid in the rescue and care of orphans, trafficking victims, and others in need of hope, vision, and purpose.

Want to Learn More About Dr. Melodye or Contact Her?

Contact her by email at:
Contact@DrMelodye.com

Visit her website at:
www.DrMelodye.com

Follow her on social media at:
https://www.facebook.com/drmelodyehilton/
www.linkedin.com/in/melodye-hilton-904b9026

Check out the VOICE OF JUSTICE FOUNDATION, Dr. Melodye Hilton's philanthropic work at: www.DrMelodye.com/voj

HILTON CONSULTING, LLC

Hilton
CONSULTING, LLC.

Learn more at www.DrMelodye.com

LEADERSHIP CONSULTING AND TRAINING

Specialized and Customized Training Topics may include:

- Justice-centric Leadership

- Validation Quotient

- Higher Living Leadership

- Higher Thinking and Emotional Hijacking

- Values-motivated Behavior

- Team-building

- Building Trust

- Conflict Resolution

- Communication

- Behavioral Consultation

- Corporate and Personal Purpose

- Shared Vision and Values

- Adapted vs. Innate Contribution

- Unmasking Prejudice

- And many more…

EXECUTIVE TEAM AND PERSONAL COACHING

CORE VALUE INDEX™ (CVI™) Dr. Melodye is a Master Certified Training for Taylor Protocols

The Most Accurate and Reliable Human Assessment Available!

A revolutionary assessment created by Taylor Protocols™ that bypasses personality and behavior revealing your unchanging motivational energies and sense for how you are wired to contribute to the world around you.

Discover your innate core values, your wired-in Human Operating System™, your six types of contribution, your negative conflict strategies, your deepest fears. With 97 percent repeat score reliability, it is stable data that is diagnostic and prescribes change. Begin your discovery of Core Values Consciousness, a new pathway to personal excellence and happiness.

This assessment is one of the simplest, most versatile tools you can find for improving an individual's self-awareness and awareness of others. If you are an employee, business owner, or someone who want to learn more about your core values, the next few minutes could positive affect you, your friends, and coworkers for years to come.

Spend less than 10 minutes and discover in your profile report:

What causes you to conflict with others;
What values you base a majority of your decisions on;
Why you make the same mistakes over and over; and
How you can improve your relationships with others.

Take a FREE CVI at: www.DrMelodye.com/cvi

Dr. Melodye is a certified behavioral consultant with the Institute of Motivational Living since 1993 and often incorporates valuable profiling tools as part of her coaching.

Some of these profiles include:

The DISC Personality Style Workbook People Keys®

This profiling instrument identifies an individual's personality style, helps him or her understand the differences in people, providing a personal review of each individual's strengths and limitations.

The Values Style Profile People Keys®

The Values Profile is Dr. Melodye Hilton's favorite profiling instrument because every aspect of an individual's life and leadership is impacted by these invisible motivators. Individuals must choose to not live by needs alone, but by values that impact their professional and personal choices of life. Values drive choices, which drive behaviors, which drive results! Conflicts arise when we hold conflicting values that determine our perception of the situations and people around us.

The TEAMS Profile People Keys®

An outstanding corporate resource for team development, this TEAMS profile will give leadership the information to strategically position each person for the greatest efficiency. The roles of Theorist, Executor, Analyzer, Manager, or Strategist are key in developing a successful work group, starting a new business, or placing people in their most natural and effective role on the team. Team members will learn their role, value to the team, core strengths, and potential limitations for each style.

VOICE OF JUSTICE FOUNDATION

Dr. Melodye Hilton's Voice of Justice Foundation is touching lives worldwide. We invite you to join us in releasing one voice for Justice!

Mission Statement:

To be a voice of hope, hands of rescue, and instruments of justice on behalf of the neglected, abused, or shamed.

Vision:

Injustice is simply an abuse of power, while justice is a righteous use of that power. The objective of the Voice of Justice Foundation is to use the influence and resources of its founders and supporters to be an instrument of justice, especially on the behalf of children and youth.

We have partnered with other not-for-profits in building schools, orphanages, and rescuing street children from abuse and prostitution. A young generation is crying out — our goal is to be an answer to its call! We are now making efforts to partner with others to see human trafficking ended and help the victims of its atrocities.

Human trafficking is the most lucrative branch of economy in the world. In contrast to drug or arms trading, humans can be sold repeatedly. The barbarity of modern slavery is taking place not only in third-world and developing countries, but in our nearest neighborhoods. Experts guess that 27 to 30 million people are victims of human trafficking worldwide.

Alarmingly, almost one-third of these are children and unfortunately, the numbers are rising.

At the time of this writing, Dr. Melodye is currently partnering with Heartwings NGO in Zurich, Switzerland. Heartwings works in the multi-cultural red-light district with a focus on humans in desperate and hopeless circumstances, who wish for a change of their situation. They wish to see dignity restored to women and children and to give them hope and help for an exit out of the devastating prison of dehumanizing slavery.

http://drmelodye.com/voj/

DISCOVER A NEW WAY OF THINKING FOR LEADERSHIP SUCCESS

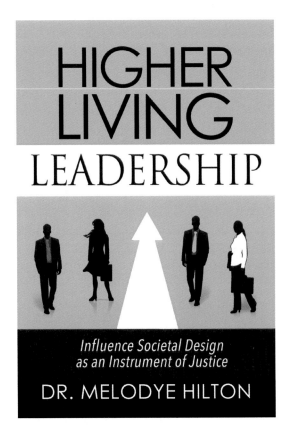

HIGHER LIVING LEADERSHIP

Influence Societal Design as an Instrument of Justice

DR. MELODYE HILTON

Through years of experience in training and consulting leaders of various spheres of influence, Dr. Melodye Hilton has developed and packaged scientifically based concepts and principles that transform the leader and their leadership application from the inside out. Presented for immediate, practical application in a marketplace setting, individuals are guided to discover their validation quotient — the attributes that unleash personal leadership value — and generate it in others to positively transform culture.

Whether leading a small family or an entire nation, this values-driven content can revolutionize the way leaders view and apply leadership. In this book, Dr. Hilton reveals the practical steps to: discover personal purpose that drives decisions and determines impact; discover and operate out of intrinsic value and be empowered to recognize it in others; recognize the effects your thoughts and choices have on the brain, body, and the fulfillment of purpose; employ Higher Thinking through continued development of the mind, purposeful choice, and values-driven self-management; and become an authentic leader who establishes trust naturally.

"In 'Higher Living Leadership', Dr. Hilton invites tomorrow's leader to think differently. Her invitation is not based on idealistic theory and philosophy, but rather, is inspired by, and rooted in real science, yet speaks to true heart of leadership and human potential." — Peter Demarest, Co-Founder, Axiogenics, LLC, and Co-Author, "Answering the Central Question"

This remarkable marketplace book shows that leadership is far more than just a title; it is a way of living. What distinguishes successful, influential, and confident leaders from the rest? The answer is "Higher Living Leadership".

Purchase: Amazon Kindle, Barnes & Nobles paperback and Nook, and iBooks

ENDORSEMENT
Higher Living Leadership

If you are an aspiring leader, or a leader who aspires to a higher level of greatness, read this book! If leadership is about unleashing human potential, not reading this book would be a great injustice to both you and all those you would lead.

At a time when fear, divisiveness, and distrust are amplifying the dark, aberrant, self-centric aspects of the collective human soul — at times when critical-thinking, personal responsibility, and moral fortitude have been buried under a blanket of political correctness, crowd-sourced morality, and a mindset of entitlement; a time when it seems that the preferred weapon against endemic injustice is even more injustice — we find a world in which the very definition of "leadership" seems to have been lost in an abyss of malpractice.

Thankfully, there are thought-leaders among us who see the current state of affairs simply as the "darkness before the dawn" and who have great wisdom to impart to those who would lead us towards a brighter future. Dr. Melodye Hilton is one of those thought-leaders.

In "Higher Living Leadership", Dr. Hilton invites tomorrow's leader to think differently. Her invitation is not based in idealistic theory and philosophy, but rather, is inspired by and rooted in real science, yet speaks to the true heart of leadership and human potential.

Peter Demarest, Author, "Answering The Central Question"
Co-Founder & President of Axiogenics, LLC
and the Self-Leadership Institute

BIBLIOGRAPHY - NOTES

Chapter 1

1. Titus, June. *Still Living, Still Learning: Meditations on Moving Beyond Loss*. Kregel, 2000.

2. "ACTS Und FACTS Zum Heartwings Verein ." *Heartwings Unite*, www.heartwings.ch/.
Peter and Dorothee' Widmer of NGO Heartwings, Zurich. Slightly rewritten because of translation with permission. http://www.heartwings.ch/

3. Spurgeon, Charles. *The Salt-Cellars: Being a Collection of Proverbs, Together with Homely Notes Thereon*. Armstrong and Son, 1889.

4. "Albert Einstein Quote." *A-Z Quotes*, www.azquotes.com/quote/87338.

Chapter 3

5. Mandela, Nelson. *Long Walk to Freedom: The Autobiography of Nelson Mandela*. Little, Brown, 1995.

6. Lieff, Jon. "Where Prejudice and Stereotypes Reside in the Brain." *Jon Lieff, M.D.*, 27 Oct. 2014, jonlieffmd.com/blog/prejudice-stereotypes-reside-brain.

7. Hilton, Melodye. *Higher Living Leadership: Influence Societal Design as an Instrument of Justice*. OUTSKIRTS Press, 2016.

Chapter 4

8. Taylor, Lynn. Personal interview. 29 October 2018
Founder of Taylor Protocols, Tukwila, WA, and creator of the Core Values Index

9. Hilton, Melodye. *Higher Living Leadership: Influence Societal Design as an Instrument of Justice*. OUTSKIRTS Press, 2016. p 20

10. Mark Arabo qtd. Boland, Barbara. "Leader: ISIS Is 'Systematically Beheading Children' in 'Christian Genocide'." *CNS News*, 9 Aug. 2014, www.cnsnews.com/mrctv-blog/barbara-boland/leader-isis-systematically-beheading-children-christian-genocide.

11. Liu, Joseph. "Rising Tide of Restrictions on Religion." *Pew Research Center's Religion & Public Life Project*, Pew Research Center , 26 Feb. 2015, www.pewforum.org/2012/09/20/rising-tide-of-restrictions-on-religion-findings/.

12. Hilton, Melodye. *Higher Living Leadership: Influence Societal Design as an Instrument of Justice*. OUTSKIRTS Press, 2016. p 24.

13. Deborah Gray White, Mia Bay, and Waldo E. Martin, Jr., *Freedom On My Mind: A History of African Americans* (Boston/New York:Bedford/ St. Martins, 2013), quoted in "Treatment of Slaves in the United States," *Wikipedia*, Accessed on 19 September 2016, wikipedia.org/wiki/Treatment_of_slaves_in_the_United_States.

14. Gashumba, Frida Umuhoza. *Frida: Chosen to Die: Destined to Live*. Sovereign World, 2007.

Chapter 5

15. Hilton, Melodye. *Higher Living Leadership: Influence Societal Design as an Instrument of Justice*. OUTSKIRTS Press, 2016. p 5

16. "The Constitution." *The White House*, The United States Government, www.whitehouse.gov/about-the-white-house/the-constitution/.

17. Watson, Benjamin. Under Our Skin: Getting Real About Race — And Getting Free from the Fears and Frustrations That Divide Us. Tyndale Momentum, 2016. page xvi

18. Hilton, Melodye. *Higher Living Leadership: Influence Societal Design as an Instrument of Justice.* Kelly Publishing, 2017. P 70, 71

19. Charles G. Finney, Memoirs (New York: A.S. Barnes, 1876), p 324. 2 Ibid, p 185-188.

Chapter 6

20. King, Jr., Martin Luther. "I Have a Dream." Washington, D.C. 28 August 1963.

21. Hilton, Melodye. *Higher Living Leadership: Influence Societal Design as an Instrument of Justice.* OUTSKIRTS Press, 2016. p 27

22. *The Bible.* The Amplified Bible, La Habra, 2015. Verse Luke 6:31.

Chapter 7

23. Labar, Kevin S, and Roberto Cabeza. "Cognitive Neuroscience of Emotional Memory." *Nature Reviews Neuroscience*, vol. 7, no. 1, 2006, pp. 54–64., doi:10.1038/nrn1825.

24. "Maya Angelou Quotes." *Largest Collection Of Maya Angelou Quotes*, www.mayaangelouquotes.org/if-we-lose-love-and-self-respect-for-each-otherthis-is-how-we-finally-die/.

25. King, Jr., Martin Luther. "Where Do We Go From Here." Annual Report Delivered at the 11th Convention of the Southern Christian Leadership Conference, Atlanta, GA. August 1967.

26. Angelou, Maya. "The Rock Cries Out Today." *The Oxford Dictionary of American Quotations* edited by Hugh Rawson and Margaret Miner, Oxford University Press, 2006, p. 317.

Ms. Angelou read the poem at the first inauguration of Pres. Bill Clinton on Jan. 20, 1993.

27. Williams, Harold. Personal interview. 27 July 2017.

28. Lebron, Nikevia. Personal interview. 26 July 2017.

29. Scott, Donna. Personal interview. 25 July 2017.

30. Ikeda, Kevin. Personal interview. 15 August 2017.

31. Ibid.

32. Monique (pseudonym). Personal interview. 24 July 2017.

33. Anna (pseudonym). Personal interview. 24 July 2017.

34. Johanna (pseudonym). Personal interview. 24 July 2017.

35. Dickens, Annette G. Personal interview. 24 July 2017.

36. Eva (pseudonym). Personal interview. 22 July 2017.

37. Johnston, Caroline. Personal interview. 29 December 2017.

38. Norman. Personal interview. 12 January 2018.

39. Weber, Ellen. "A Brain on Forgiveness." Brain Leaders And Learners, 27 Aug. 2018, brainleadersandlearners.com/2018/08/27/a-brain-on-forgiveness/.

40. Eva (pseudonym). Personal interview. 22 July 2017.

Chapter 8

41. "White Christmas is a 1954 American musical romantic comedy film directed by Michael Curtiz and starring Bing Crosby, Danny Kaye, Rosemary Clooney, and Vera-Ellen. Filmed in VistaVision and Technicolor, it features the songs of Irving Berlin, including a new version of the title song, 'White Christmas'..." https://en.wikipedia.org/wiki/White_Christmas_(film)

42. Emily (pseudonym). Personal interview. 22 August 2017.

43. Ibid.

Chapter 9

44. Hilton, Melodye. *Higher Living Leadership: Influence Societal Design as an Instrument of Justice*. OUTSKIRTS Press, 2016. P 98-99

Chapter 10

1 "Martin Luther King, Jr. Quotes." *BrainyQuote*, Xplore, www.brainyquote.com/quotes/martin_luther_king_jr_717840.

45. King, Martin Luther, and Coretta Scott King. Where Do We Go from Here: Chaos or Community? Beacon Press, 2010.

46. "The Bill of Rights: A Transcription." National Archives and Records Administration, National Archives and Records Administration, www.archives.gov/founding-docs/bill-of-rights-transcript.

47. Duez, Traci. "Improving Your Reality ." Breaking Free , Break Free Consulting, Nov. 2008, www.breakfreeconsulting.com/newsletter/200811-improving_reality.htm.

Chapter 11

48. King, Martin Luther. "Letter from Birmingham Jail." *African Studies Center*, University of Pennsylvania, www.africa.upenn.edu/Articles_Gen/Letter_Birmingham.html.

Chapter 12

49. [1] Mandela, Nelson. *The Illustrated Long Walk to Freedom: the Autobiography of Nelson Mandela*. Little, Brown, 2008. Originally published 1995.

50. [2] Weber, Ellen. "A Brain on Forgiveness." Brain Leaders And Learners, 27 Aug. 2018, brainleadersandlearners.com/2018/08/27/a-brain-on-forgiveness/.

51. [3] Ibid.

52. Smedes, Lewis B. *The Art of Forgiving: When You Need to Forgive and Don't Know How.* Ballantine Books, 1997, p. 178.

53. Leaf, Caroline. *Who Switched off My Brain? Controlling toxic thoughts and emotions.* Series # 4, DVD. Dallas, TX.

54. Weber, Ellen. "A Brain on Forgiveness." Brain Leaders And Learners, 27 Aug. 2018, brainleadersandlearners.com/2018/08/27/a-brain-on-forgiveness/.

55. Dr. Melodye Hilton, *Higher Living Leadership: Influence Societal Design as an Instrument of Justice.* OUTSKIRTS Press, 2017, p. 8, 4-85

56. King, Martin Luther. *Measure of a Man / by Martin Luther King, Jr.* Martino Fine Books, 2013. Originally published 1959.

Chapter 13

57. Lieberman, Matthew qtd in Rock, David. "Managing with the Brain in Mind." *Strategy+Business*, PwC, 27 Aug. 2009, www.strategy-business.com/article/09306?gko=5df7f.

58. Demarest, Peter D., and Harvey J. Schoof. *Answering the Central Question; How Science Reveals the Keys to Success in Life, Love, and Leadership.* HeartLead Publishing, 2010. P. 47-48.

59. Lash, Joseph P., *Helen and Teacher: The Story of Helen Keller and Anne Sullivan Mac.* Delacorte Press, 1980, p. 489.

60. Mandela, Nelson. *The Illustrated Long Walk to Freedom: the Autobiography of Nelson Mandela.* Little, Brown, 2008. Originally published 1995.

61. King, Jr., Martin Luther. "Rediscovering Lost Values." Second Baptist Church, 28 February 1954, Detroit MI. Sermon.

62. "13 Of Maya Angelou's Best Quotes." Edited by Lindsay Deutsch, USA Today, USA Today Network, 28 May 2014, www.usatoday.com/story/news/nation-now/2014/05/28/maya-angelou-quotes/9663257/.

63. Unknown

64. Angelou, Maya. *Rainbow in the Cloud: the Wisdom and Spirit of Maya Angelou.* Random House, 2014, p.12.

65. qtd. In Baxter, Rod. *Cultural Engagement for Success Handbook.* Value Generation Partners, LLC, 2016, P. 39.

66. Covey, Stephen R. *The 7 Habits of Highly Effective People Powerful Lessons in Personal Change.* Simon & Schuster, 2013. p. 229-230.

Conclusion

67. Demarest, Peter D., and Harvey J. Schoof. *Answering the Central Question; How Science Reveals the Keys to Success in Life, Love, and Leadership.* HeartLead Publishing, 2010. P. 4.

68. Ibid. P. 47.

69. Unknown

Over the years, we have adopted a number of dogs from rescues and shelters. First there was Bear and after he passed, Ginger and Scout. Now, we have Kira, another rescue. They have brought immense joy and love not just into our lives, but into the lives of all who met them.

We want you to know a portion of the profits of this book will be donated in Bear, Ginger and Scout's memory to local animal shelters, parks, conservation organizations, and other individuals and nonprofit organizations in need of assistance.

— *Douglas & Sherri Brown*,
President & Vice-President of Atlantic Publishing